The Poetry of
DAVID SHAPIRO

The Poetry of DAVID SHAPIRO

Thomas Fink

Rutherford • Madison • Teaneck
Fairleigh Dickinson University Press
London and Toronto: Associated University Presses

© 1993 by Associated University Presses, Inc.

All rights reserved. Authorization to photocopy items for internal or personal use, or the internal or personal use of specific clients, is granted by the copyright owner, provided that a base fee of $10.00, plus eight cents per page, per copy is paid directly to the Copyright Clearance Center, 27 Congress Street, Salem, Massachusetts 01970. [0-8386-3495-8/92 $10.00+8¢ pp, pc.]

Associated University Presses
440 Forsgate Drive
Cranbury, NJ 08512

Associated University Presses
25 Sicilian Avenue
London WC1A 2QH, England

Associated University Presses
P.O. Box 39, Clarkson Pstl. Stn.
Mississauga, Ontario,
L5J 3X9 Canada

The paper used in this publication meets the requirements of the American National Standard for Permanence of Paper for Printed Library Materials Z39.48-1984.

Library of Congress Cataloging-in-Publication Data

Fink, Thomas.
    The poetry of David Shapiro / Thomas Fink.
      p. cm.
    ISBN 0-8386-3495-8 (alk. paper)
    1. Shapiro, David, 1947– —Criticism and interpretation.
I. Title.
PS3569.H34Z68   1993
811'.54—dc20   91-58946
                                                                         CIP

PRINTED IN THE UNITED STATES OF AMERICA

To Molly Mason
and Ariana Mason Fink

Contents

Acknowledgments	9
Introduction	13
1. Thresholds of Readability: The Disjunctive Collage-Poems	37
2. Desire, Representation, and Critique	50
3. "Mirrors Rushing into Each Other": The Poetics of Eros	68
4. "The Pluralism of Possible Styles": A Reading of "The Devil's Trill Sonata"	88
Conclusion	111
Notes	115
Bibliography	118
Index	121

Acknowledgments

Grateful acknowledgment is made to David Shapiro for permission to quote from his books, *January* (New York: Holt, Rinehart and Winston, 1965); *Poems from Deal* (New York: E. P. Dutton, 1969); *A Man Holding an Acoustic Panel* (New York: E. P. Dutton, 1971); and *John Ashbery: An Introduction to the Poetry* (New York: Columbia University Press, 1979), and to quote the entirety of his poems, "After a Lost Original" and "You Are Tall and Thin," which are parts of the long poem, "After a Lost Original," to be published as a chapbook by Solo Press, 1992.

Quotations from *To an Idea* by David Shapiro, © 1983 by David Shapiro, published by the Overlook Press, Lewis Hollow Road, Woodstock, N.Y. 12498, are reprinted by permission of the publisher.

Quotations from *Lateness* by David Shapiro, © 1977 by David Shapiro, published by the Overlook Press, Lewis Hollow Road, Woodstock, N.Y. 12498, are reprinted by permission of the publisher.

Quotations from *House (Blown Apart)* by David Shapiro, © 1988 by David Shapiro, published by the Overlook Press, Lewis Hollow Road, Woodstock, N.Y. 12498, are reprinted by permission of the publisher.

Quotations from *The Page-Turner* (New York: Liveright Publishing Corporation, 1973) are reprinted by permission of the publisher.

Quotations from *The Collected Poems of Wallace Stevens* by Wallace Stevens are reprinted by permission of Alfred A. Knopf, Inc.

I would also like to express my appreciation to Paul Bove, John Chu, John Haber, Edward Davenport, Shivaji Sengupta, Stephen Paul Miller, Tuzyline Allan, and Judith Halden-Sullivan, all of whom have contributed to my understanding of the theory and practice of literary criticism through many invaluable dialogues, and to David Shapiro for his gracious assistance.

The Poetry of
DAVID SHAPIRO

Introduction

I

David Shapiro opens his poem "Star" with the line, "You have to kneel down on your hands, to sue Life for all it's worth" (MHAP, 61).[1] Relentlessly experimental, Shapiro has labored for three decades and through seven books to sue poetry for all it is worth: to turn previous modes of writing inside out, to stretch them beyond recognition, to scorch them at times, and to demand (and attain) vibrant new poetic opportunities. Not only do many fresh and intricate poetic forms populate his poetry, but he continually probes varying degrees of thematic continuity and discontinuity, precise reference and polysemy, self-reference and thwarted attempts at making meaning. As befits a professional musician's work, subtle, complex, and often unpredictable tonal shifts abound. Full of agile intellectual humor but never motivated by whimsy, Shapiro's experimentation stems from a passionate impulse to break arbitrary limitations, to think in and through poetry by doubting and—to cite the title of one poem of the late 1980s—by "doubting the doubts" (HBA, 59).[2]

Experimental poets are frequently labeled "obscurantist" by readers who do not wish to take the time to shelve prejudices for a while and read slowly and painstakingly. Given the abundance of interesting (experimental and "traditional") contemporary poets, most of whom pose smaller obstacles to speedy understanding, one can understand why these readers develop principles of exclusion and can even empathize with their need to do so. If some literary experimenters pursue novelty and obscurity for specious reasons—for example, simply to "make it new" without regard for the particular value of their novelty—in Shapiro's case, the label "obscurantist" is unmerited. First of all, his poetry often evinces an appreciation of simple and complex lucidities, as in the recurrent fascination with snow: "Since I was born in the city of Newark / Moment by moment a very fine snow has been falling. / On very few days has it stopped snowing in my sleep" (*TI*, 63).³ Second, as citations from his literary and art critical writings indicate, he believes that forms of discontinuity enable one to resist *false* clarities, which, after all, obscure a great deal. Acknowledging in "Doubting the Doubts" that "We all love clarity," the speaker continues: "But you love darkness. / But darkness is clear" (*HBA*, 59). Shapiro "loves darkness" *when* it clarifies something.

Although his work has been praised—at various stages in his career—by such authoritative literary figures as Jack Kerouac, Kay Boyle, Jerome McGann, Frank O'Hara, John Ashbery, Kenneth Koch, Harold Bloom, and Philip Lopate, Shapiro has not received adequate critical attention. Not only does his poetry deserve sustained consideration because of the rich variety of his experiments, but close attention to his persistent, purposeful, and various challenges to the protocols of textual understanding can contribute to the exploration of a central concern of contemporary critical theory: the general discussion of the problematics of reading. In reviewing *To an Idea* (1983), Jorie Graham states: "Mr. Shapiro thinks of every reader as a 'writing reader,' and because he often refuses to make certain choices about meaning, he compels us to make them."⁴ While I believe that Shapiro would concur with the first point, the cause/effect relationship in the second is highly questionable. The refusal to write poems in which "certain [determinate] choices about meaning" seem plausible—much less, inevitable—may indicate that the poet wants the reader to resist the "compulsion" to make immediate choices and to think about what makes it so difficult to choose. Thus, in reading Shapiro, one should often turn to examine, modify, and perhaps dislodge the theoretical presuppositions that one had brought to the reading process. As Barbara Johnson notes in the "Opening Remarks" of her book *The Critical Difference*, "Theoretical pronouncements . . . do not stand . . . as instruments to be used in mastering literary structures. On the contrary, it is through contact with literature that theoretical tools are useful precisely to the extent that they thereby change and dissolve in the hands of the user."¹⁵

II

At the end of his pioneering study of John Ashbery's poetry (1979), David Shapiro presents a terse biographical note and appends a justification for leaving "the factual life in a corner." Like Wallace Stevens, he wishes

> to delete the vulgar notion of biography from poetry. I agree, however, with Jakobson, that a "vulgar anti-biographism" should not rule. I have tried to import my knowledge of Ashbery's temperament and character into all possible moments of my analysis. But a poem is not merely or primarily the consciousness of its author—it is a dynamism, a dissemination, a scattering of screens. (JA, 177–78).[6]

For Shapiro and Ashbery, "the vulgar notion of biography [in] poetry" may conjure up a specific historical referent. During the 1960s, Shapiro's formative years as a poet, so-called "Confessional Poetry" was widely acclaimed, and his own "New York School" mentors, O'Hara, Koch, and Ashbery, who saw themselves in opposition to both "Confessional Poetry" and "cooked" academic formalism, were comparatively neglected. While Frank O'Hara took most of his poetic material from personal experience, the poetry does not amount to "confession"; it reflects the unruly, multicontexted flux of his experience. In his master's thesis at City College of New York (1983) comparing Shapiro and Jasper Johns, Stephen Paul Miller notes, "Shapiro adapts O'Hara's use of personal associations but deletes from them all hint of what they refer to. . . . The poem and process of writing a poem are emphasized over anything the poem describes."[7]

From time to time, Shapiro does supply hints of what his autobiographical associations might refer to, but they never add up to anything like Robert Lowell's thorough unveiling of his parents' inadequacies and his own bouts with mental illness in *Life Studies*. For Shapiro, then, the poet's personality and personal history are a *part* of the many interactive elements of poetry, but he believes that they have been overemphasized in much postwar American poetry, to the detriment of other vital concerns—for example, the limitations inherent in the structuring of language and in conventions of linguistic use that hinder attempts to represent the self.

For Shapiro's readers, it seems important to avoid both "the vulgar notion of biography" and "vulgar antibiographism." Thus, in interpreting Shapiro's poetry, I will accord biographical detail a small role. And yet, I will now give a moderately detailed account of certain events of his life that seem to impinge—to varying degrees—on the choices he has made as a poet and on the contexts of his poetic production.

Born on 2 January 1947 in Newark, New Jersey, Shapiro was deeply influenced by close family members at a very early age to immerse himself in literature and music. His maternal grandfather, Berele Chagy, was a noted cantor and composer. His mother, Frieda, considered an extremely promising classical singer in her youth, was well acquainted with close friends of Auden and Spender in the South African literary community. His uncle, John Chagy, a pianist, published poems in the *New York Times*. Irving Shapiro, David's father, is a physician who studied sculpture with one of Rodin's students, makes portrait busts, and has always read literature voraciously. Between the ages of four and ten, David Shapiro read and memorized sizeable chunks of the writings of Milton, Shakespeare, and Blake, and at ten, he took great pride in memorizing Eliot's *The Waste Land*.

By his fifth birthday, it was evident that Shapiro was a violin prodigy. In "On Becoming a Person," the speaker states, "In a sense, we are all child prodigies" (*PT*, 36).[8] At five, he appeared on the "Voice of America" program, and, in the next eleven years, he performed with several orchestras, most notably the New Jersey Symphony and (at sixteen) the American Symphony, in which he played violin under the redoubtable Leopold Stokowski.

At nine, Shapiro wrote his first poem. For the next seven years, he spent one to three hours a day writing poetry. He began publishing abroad at the age of ten, and his first American publication came in 1960 (in the *Antioch Review*). Driven to succeed as a poet, he haunted the Newark Public Library, one of the first and best open-stack public libraries in the East coast, and tried to read every book in the poetry section. Oppressed by the experience of constant performance as a violinist and by the fear that the endless practice was turning him into a "trained monkey," Shapiro perceived poetry as freedom—the opposite of performance. He knew that family members wanted him to become a leading violinist, but he longed to devote himself primarily to poetry, especially when more and more poems were being accepted for publication.

In 1962, one of Shapiro's high school teachers enabled him to represent his school as a participant at the Wagner College Writer's Conference in New York City. At the conference, Kenneth Koch, the teacher of Shapiro's workshop, was astounded by the quality of the high school poet's work and immediately sent some of it to John Ashbery (who was living in Paris at the time) for publication in the first issue of the magazine *Art and Literature*. Shapiro also met Frank O'Hara at the conference, and afterward he left his poems for O'Hara to read at the latter's Museum of Modern Art office. Without telling him, O'Hara gave some of the poems to Diane DePrima for publication in *Floating Bear*.

Shapiro had encountered the work of all three "New York School" poets in Donald Allen's celebrated anthology, *The New American Poetry* (1960), and had been dazzled by Ashbery's radical experimentation. The young man quickly became a protégé of both Koch and O'Hara. Not only did both poets engage him in many discussions of poetic craft, but they introduced him to some of the major New York painters of the era, including Fairfield Porter and Jasper Johns. In addition, John Ashbery wrote Shapiro several extremely encouraging letters from Paris before he returned to live in New York in 1965.

When Shapiro was still in high school, Holt, Rinehart and Winston accepted *January*, his first book, which appeared in 1965. In an unpublished interview that I conducted in 1989, the poet recalls:

January was published because the Jewish theologian Arthur A. Cohen wrote to me after seeing poems in *Art and Literature*. He was very brave to publish such a young person. Reviews were mixed. I didn't want to publish a book, I told Kenneth [Koch], until it was perfect and I was forty and Stevens-like. He told me that was nonsense; there was no perfect time, and I could help other poets. I then proceeded to try to convert Arthur to Kenneth, John [Ashbery], and O'Hara.

Among those who wrote advance comments for the book were

Ashbery, Kay Boyle, Jack Kerouac, Koch, and Kenneth Rexroth. *January* includes love poems, family poems, and quasi-mystical moments, as in the beginning of "Canticle":

> I was on a white coast once.
> My father was with me on his head.
> I said:
> Father, father, I can't fall down.
> I was born for the sun and the moon.
> I looked at the clouds
> and all the clouds were mounting.
> My friends made a blue ring.
> O we hung down with the birds.[9]
>
> (J, 9).

Noting that poems like "Canticle" are "relatively conventional when compared to Shapiro's later work," Stephen Paul Miller writes:

The earliest poetry we have of his can be likened to an expressive surrealism. Shapiro would then tend most often to write about a subject from an emotional perspective, usually displaying contradictory feelings toward his subject, a poetic and inner analogue to the Cubist vision. These poems stuck to a particular scene, albeit they may have changed almost every element in that scene.[10]

The same year that *January* was published, Shapiro received the Breadloaf Writers Conference Robert Frost Fellowship. What was a strong probability two years earlier, when he played under Stokowski, was now established: poetry would be his major pursuit, and the violin would be a secondary activity. For three of his four undergraduate years at Columbia, Shapiro played in the Columbia Symphony, often as lead violinist, and he has played in various concerts since then, most recently at Saint Mark's Church in Manhattan and on a local radio station. But, in a sense, the prodigy grew up to "renounce" music. "Falling Upwards" (1983) speaks of such a renunciation:

> A certain violinist had a beautiful violin
> But before he had time to play her long and listen
> To her tones as such, he was compelled to renounce music

And sell her, and go on a far journey, and leave his violin in the
   hands of the violin case. . . .

What was there to do. It is said you cannot live your life in your
   room and not go out.
What was there to do? It is said music disobeys
And reaches the prince's courtyard farther than smell and grits its
   notes like teeth and gives us food and drink.
And orders a fire to be lighted, famished silk to hang over it and
   repetitions to be sharpened.

What was there to do? It is said it is the violinists who do not sleep.
What was there to do? It is said we think and don't think; we are
   asleep.
What was there to do? It is said music sinks into the mire up to its
   neck, wants to crawl out, but cannot.
What was there to do? It is said the violin was a swan, seized the
   boy, falling upwards to some height above the earth.
(TI, 11)

More than almost any of Shapiro's poems, "Falling Upwards" tempts the reader to practice "vulgar biographism." There is more than a taste of "recollection in agitation" here. "Compelled to renounce music" and "go on a far journey" (in the unchartered territory of poetry?), the protagonist, whose "story" is conveyed to us by an unidentified narrator, fears that a professional violinist must "live [his] life in [his] room and not go out"—too obsessed with practice to sleep and yet "asleep" because he misses too much of life. Nevertheless, one should hesitate before swallowing the biographical bait. Failing to include specific references to poetry as an alternative, the poem is full of surreal fantasy that could not refer to Shapiro's concrete situation. In the striking, paradoxical image of the swan-violin "seiz[ing] the boy," one might interpret the boy as being rescued from something like the fate of Icarus (being burned by the sun) during his "upward falling" flight "to some height above the earth." And yet, "seized" might have the more negative connotation of "violent possession"; the violin might have been rudely interrupting a *delightfully* uncontrollable flight of the imagination. Does the boy approve of being "seized"? Does the violin cancel his prior renunciation? We are not told.

The oft-reiterated phrase, "it is said," suggests that any one of many aphorisms and pseudoaphorisms about music and violinists may or may not be true. If music involves monastic discipline and "grits its notes like teeth," it is also considered a "disobedient" liberator that "gives us food and drink," exquisite pleasures, and, like Prometheus, "orders a fire to be lighted." Although " it is said music sinks into the mire up to its neck" and cannot "crawl out," the next "saying" contradicts it, since the violin has risen way above the mire. Whereas "confessional poetry" usually depends on a clear exposition of basic facts and a tacit understanding of a hierarchy of values, Shapiro gives us neither. Instead, utilizing traces of autobiographical material, he rapidly presents and questions various attitudes about music—without endorsing any—and considers how one can and cannot calculate the gains and losses of any pursuit of the "sublime."

Shapiro perpetuates his affirmation and practice of music in his poetry with formal achievements ("repetitions to be sharpened") and with demonstrations that the auditory performance of words can override the force of their conventional denotations. Since the displacement of desire from music to poetry has been an important theme in his life, one might suspect that this situation has attracted the poet to the general problem of displacement and the complex interplay of absence and presence that "inhabits" a substantial aspect of his mature poetry. Although his "career decision" may have influenced this part of his poetry somewhat, I sense that there are numerous other influences as well, some of which should emerge in the rest of this book.

When Shapiro was a freshman at Columbia, President Lyndon Johnson, enjoying a landslide victory over Barry Goldwater in the 1964 presidential election, used his "mandate" to escalate U.S. participation in the Vietnam War. Shapiro's parents were left-wing community activists, and so he was accustomed at an early age to involvement in political causes. An early member of SANE, the antinuclear organization, he considered himself a pacifist and joined in the many campus protests of what he has called the "imperial war" and of Columbia University's alliance with the defense industry.

In April 1968, the wave of protests at Columbia reached its apex with the student takeover of Low Library, the university's chief administrative building. In an 13 October 1969 article entitled "Where Are They Now?" Shapiro's participation in this act of "guerilla theater" is chronicled in *Newsweek*, a leading "establishment" magazine. The article singles out the "striking" and "widely reprinted" photograph of Shapiro: "a mustached, long-haired young man sitting in Grayson Kirk's chair and puffing one of the Columbia president's cigars during the April 1968 occupation of Low Library. . . . [T]o many older Americans, it symbolized everything they felt to be reprehensible about the emerging radicals, including their disregard for private property."[11]

Identifying himself as "more of a poet than an activist (he was not an SDS member)," Shapiro is quoted in the article as saying: "'I saw the occupation of the administration building as "logical revolt," and also traditionally American. . . . What I was deliberately trying to do was to parody the elite, gang, clique, cabal, club,' Shapiro . . . says of the famous picture. 'This is the technique of parody—I don't smoke cigars.'"[12]

The 7 June 1968 cover story of *Time*, "Cynical Idealists of '68," relates Shapiro's response to a "massive police raid at" Columbia. The poet "walked into the office of the Columbia College dean, ripped up his new Phi Beta Kappa certificate, and said, 'I'm ashamed of this university.'" The article also attributes these statements to him:

"The struggle is for each man to live up to his own conscience, even if it is under continual pressure to go to sleep. The whole world is being divided into those that are participating in the waking up and those that would massage and tranquilize."

To adults who criticize the tactics students employed at Columbia, Shapiro asks: "What are the techniques that the liberals are suggesting? I don't hear them in a time of crisis. I think one thing that youth has on its side is a feeling of crisis. Most of the intellectuals in this country have abdicated their critical role or are being sentimentalists."[13]

Shapiro has told me that he did not join the SDS because, as a pacifist, he felt uneasy about the "menacing infantilism" of the group's leadership. He saw the distinct possibility that their protest would turn violent. Nevertheless, he called himself a "fellow traveler" of the group. His public statements—perhaps, he believes, slightly misquoted by *Time* and *Newsweek* to make them even more confrontational than they were—contain the fervent, polarizing, anticomformist, and yet collectivist rhetoric characteristic of numerous student "radicals" of the period. (They also have a touch of the avant-garde poet's sense of parodic irony.) Over twenty years later, Shapiro remembers that, as a senior who had just earned the prestigious Kellett Fellowship for graduate study in literature at Cambridge University, he understood the substantial risk he was taking but felt driven by a sense of social urgency, and, possibly, an impulse to destroy what he had gained. In these interviews of the late 1960s, Shapiro seemed to believe that he had to adopt a political voice (outside his poetry) that could produce a resoundingly direct communication in the context of the mass media. When *Time* interviewed him for a retrospective feature article in 1986, he had obviously developed a great deal of suspicion about the implications of such rhetoric, and so he spoke with a good deal more caution.

Reading the poems of *January* and *Poems from Deal* (1969), published when the poet was a graduate student at Clare College, Cambridge, I do not find even a bare outline of the radical's Romantic rhetoric. In fact, there are only a handful of fragmentary political references and only two overtly political poems, "Dirge (South Africa)" (*J*, 27), which speaks puzzlingly about apartheid, and "Irresistible Poison" (*PD*, 48),[14] which swerves away from allusions to "The Russo-American minuet," "The Arab-Israeli war," and the civil rights struggle ("the clouds over Glassboro") in the last two of five quatrains, in order to describe a love relationship.

In Shapiro's two books of the 1980s, there have been a greater number of sociopolitical references and implications in the poems, with some strong *hints* of social protest, but very little direct political rhetoric and no sustained, unified political critique. Shapiro mistrusts such political discursiveness (as well as the journalistic reportage that often goes with it) in poetry, since this kind of language often falls into the very authoritarianism that it is intended to dispute. In my interview with him, he said:

I have thought that a certain amount of Trotzkyite freedom should exist before, during, and after the revolution. I've wanted the guarantees of privacy to be part of any libertarian mode, and I've been very skeptical of Marxian movements both in and out of the university that seem to be dogmatic and unresponsive to pluralist, tolerant goals.

In many of Shapiro's poems, one can interpret the use of what the Russian Formalists called "de-familiarization" as a resistance to the degraded language of false collectivity (conformism) that characterizes much mass communication and the pronouncements of those in the American political establishment. The experimental poet creates a "pocket" of freedom by expanding both the possibilities of personal expression and shared linguistic experience. In the *Time* article of 19 May 1986, Shapiro speaks of poetic activity as a kind of "infiltration" and poetry as "an insidious private language, yielding an alternative to the public language of TIME magazine and TV. My art is intervention. My method is doubt." But he calls "the system . . . wildly stronger than my tiny interventions. It's hard to numb the hand of the American empire."[15] Poetry, then, is meant to serve a collective deposition of authoritarian "public" forces. In addition, the critique of various forms of representation (to be found in Shapiro's poetry of the 1980s) can be considered an indirect way of challenging authoritarian uses of myths and other structures that pretend to provide total explanations of complex phenomena.

Shapiro's second book, *Poems from Deal*, moves away from what Stephen Paul Miller calls the "relatively conventional" aspect of *January* and jumps into the wild experiments with disjunction (through collage), surreal imagery, and tonal variety that characterize much of the poet's best work of the 1970s. Poems such as the goofily hyperbolic "Seraphita," "The Human Voice," and parts of the longer "In Memory of Your Body" mark advances in Shapiro's exploration of the possibilities of erotic poetry. The surreal, prose-poetic "inventory" of a lover's body in the last-named poem is especially striking:

Your body has narrow slits instead of windows. And inside, your brain turns around, silent. The more mouth you have the more pleasure. Your eyes look like stables, look like dungeons, though they are hard and white, of course, as your legs. Nor are those legs without ornament: Two chains of great size and rotundity keep you prisoner. Loitering on the beach, one common night, they were recognized and stopped. In another corner of your body, a fountain spouts. (*PD*, 17)

In poems like "Tracks," "Poems from Deal," and "Master Canterel at Locus Solus," which are each divided into several short sections, Shapiro presents fragmentary allusions to "real experience" but violently expunges transitions and, hence, ferociously resists overall thematic interpretation. As in Ashbery's poetry, abrupt pronoun shifts abound:

> She puts the mural on you lightly
> where horse and ceiling meet.
> Excitement can be measured by analysis
> and I'm far away on a sofa.
>
> Once I was so desperate
> to carve down an adorable work,
> I couldn't reopen it later on
> even with a (lazy) business-suit on.
>
> You are playing with the waves
> and swimming theatrically.
>
> ("Tracks," *PD*, 40)

Reviewing *Poems from Deal* in the October 1970 issue of *Poetry*, philosopher and poet John Koethe calls the book "a real advance" over *January*, praises Shapiro for his "incredible mastery of the language and an ear sensitive to every nuance of idiom and rhythm," and stresses the work's "musical" quality, "for the poems seem to flow in a continuous wave which the poet gently modulates rather than consciously orders." Koethe lucidly describes the "defamiliarizing" impact of Shapiro's most "difficult" poems:

His power stems from his ability to ride the tide of the language and then suddenly thwart, both metrically and semantically, the expectations this induces in us. This polarization of language has the effect of transforming entire lines and phrases into meaningless blocks of words where, paradoxically, each word seems to vibrate with the bewitching fiction of its "essential meaning."[16]

I would only quarrel with Koethe's use of the word "meaningless," because individual phrases and sentences do yield meanings, while connections among different "blocks of words" are deleted. When Koethe speaks of "the fiction of [an] essential meaning," he may be suggesting that the reader learns to get past discomfort with the absence of connections and to derive significance from a sense of how words have properties independent of their status as "stand-ins" for nonverbal experience.

As an M.A. student at Cambridge (1968–70), Shapiro concentrated heavily on the interdisciplinary study of literature and art. Early in his stay, he received a letter from the noted editor and art writer Thomas Hess, whom he had met through Ashbery, asking him—since he was living in Great Britain—to write the first essay on David Hockney's art for *Art News*. Not only did Shapiro comply, but he became a regular art writer for the magazine, eventually reaching the position of editorial assistant. In the past twenty years, he has also written art criticism for *Art in America*, the *New Yorker*, *Craft Horizons*, *Arts*, and various other journals, as well as a number of catalog essays, including *Poets and Painters: Lines of Color*. In his art criticism, Shapiro makes extensive interdisciplinary connections between art, literature, philosophy, psychology, critical theory, and architecture. (In 1970, upon his return from England, he married Lindsay Stamm, an architect, designer, and architecture professor who co-edited the architecture series, *Oppositions*, published concurrently by the Institute for Architecture and Urban Studies and the MIT Press.)

Shapiro is the author of books of art criticism on Jasper Johns, Jim Dine, and Piet Mondrian, and he has written substantial essays for various others. When I asked him about Jasper Johns's influence on his poetry and poetics during our 1989 interview, Shapiro said:

For a long time, Johns has been one of my aesthetic standards. He might be amused by the fact that I think of him as a ruler or a standard, and it is probably absurd. It's very much part of his work to find absurd using someone as a ruler or standard. . . . When I was working on an article on Jasper Johns, "The World Map," I became intrigued again by his underlining of his taste for "disastrous relationships." He said that Buckminster Fuller preferred clear information; he [Johns] preferred "disastrous relationships," and I watched him repaint "The World Map." He permitted me to paint Cook Island, a detail. I was interested in the humor of Johns' repainting of the world map in arbitrary colors, disastrously different than Fuller's positivist colors.

In keeping with the playful references to "ruler," "standard," and "map" as problematic tools of measurement in Johns, the poet's book on the painter offers trenchant formulations about the complexities of representation in art. Shapiro especially appreciates Johns's efforts to "perturb," "dislocate," and "unhinge" facile unifying structures in order to achieve a more powerful heterogeneity of effects:

In Jasper Johns, the hand is a kind of voice. Where others draw persons, things, and objects, he draws intrinsicality. Each mark of Johns is a disagreement, a contradistinction, a modification of the mood. Johns' drawings are not preparations; they are perturbations. They do not so much study and organize as dislocate and unhinge. . . . Johns has a lover's quarrel with the real. He loves to differ and discover; therefore he draws. . . . In him, drawing is a suffix, an alternative, a prolongation of thinking by other means.[17]

Shapiro's recent study of Mondrian's early work treats the problem of representation in a different way from the Johns's text; here, Shapiro is concerned with subtle antagonisms between Mondrian's theory and practice. In our interview, he notes:

Mondrian's flowers obsessively interested me, because of the example of what seemed to be the libidinous in a work that elsewhere tabooed the libido. . . . If one does reduce to "zero degree," it should be for further heat, as I think Ashbery and other good reductivists have known. Mondrian's flowers to me provide wonderful ways in which one can demonstrate how horribly modernist theory can go against its own practitioners. I think that Mondrian had boxed himself into a corner at times, and the flowers and the abstract paintings themselves are better than the corner he theoretically boxed himself into.

While Shapiro notes in this interview that his own poetry is "friendly to theory," he is also aware that poetry and its reception would be impoverished by *submitting* it to a rigid theoretical program: "Practically, I have been involved in how poetry could both underline what Jacobsen called 'the grammar of poetry and the poetry of grammar,' and yet also one wants a poetry that is not dogmatically chaste." This seems a warning to critics to avoid reading Shapiro's work as a "pure" example of the tenets of a particular "school" of critical theory.

To return to the year 1970 and to the notion of a different kind of "school," Shapiro co-edited *An Anthology of New York Poets* with Ron Padgett. Not only did the anthology contain work by "senior members" of the "school" but poetry by a broad selection of younger writers. Many poets and critics have discussed the inadequacies of the term "New York School of Poetry," which—despite Padgett and Shapiro's disclaimer in the anthology's introduction that the "school" was heterogeneous and held no dogma—has been used to lump together writers with diverse aims and label them whimsical, undisciplined parodists. Not only are O'Hara, Koch, and Ashbery playfully serious in their best writing, but their thematic concerns and some of their stylistic traits are markedly different from one another. While Shapiro shares a severe skepticism about absolutes, a use of multiple tones and collage techniques, and an openness to surreal imagery with these older poets, he is more concerned with the investigation of various modes of representation than O'Hara and Koch, writes more directly about sexual love than Ashbery, and includes the theme of family much more frequently than all three. In addition, Shapiro differ significantly with his "elders" in his uses of tone and his unique intellectual wit. While political positions seem largely absent from the poetry of O'Hara, Koch, and Ashbery, who have not engaged in the kind of political activism that Shapiro has, the latter offers fragmentary criticisms of oppression in such poems as "To the Earth," "To a Young Exile," "Work in Sadness," and "A Fragile Art," as well as in several long poems.

Shapiro's third book of poetry, *A Man Holding an Acoustic Panel* (1971), was nominated for the National Book Award. The long (eighteen section) title-poem includes surreal moments of danger, hints of family history in a context of current uncertainty, disjunctive "losses scattered erratically in the sky" (16), the dizzying experience of synesthesia, "the lottery of heredity" (27), and a brief, moving political elegy. The poem, which (the poet has mentioned) continually moves among several geographical scenes, can be read as a "catalog" of defamiliarizations, of perturbations that refuse mastery. Often, Shapiro makes disruptive external forces seem inexorable, as in the first "subpoem," "The Danube Loophole":

On the ship there is an international airport.

> Here, their passports are taken away from them.
>
> These walls, these acoustical bricks, protect the man holding an acoustical panel against a wave of shock and sound.
>
> Ordinary microphones don't hear it, only the microphones with "great surface" permit us to—Walls and closets will not stop it—we will take these sounds to our grave.
>
> Hearts working with determined frequency like twenty hearts,
>   hands
> black as glands.
>
> (MHAP, 11)

A Man Holding an Acoustic Panel also contains several impressive shorter poems. I have already mentioned the surreal elegance of "Star." "Fire and Life" memorably represents a chaos of body sensations within a collage of fractured narratives. "The Carburetor at Venice" articulates a masterfully deranged flirtation, while "Necessity" and "Ode to Visibility" are more calmly meditative poems. Shapiro also includes two striking surreal collaborations with children whom he had taught in elementary school writing workshops. In the collaborations of that period, he was influenced by the teaching of Kenneth Koch, who used it, as Shapiro noted to me in our unpublished interview, "as an antiromantic or surrealist device for taking oneself by surprise."

Upon his return to New York in late 1970, Shapiro enrolled in the doctoral program in the Columbia English department. In 1972, he became an instructor in the department, and upon completion of his Ph.D. the next year, an assistant professor, a post he held until 1980. Under the supervision of John Unterecker, a noted scholar of modernist poetry, Shapiro wrote the first doctoral dissertation on John Ashbery, and Columbia University Press later published a revised version in book form.

While Harold Bloom, the first critic to devote significant attention to Ashbery, had perceived the poet's middle volume, *The Double Dream of Spring*, as the point at which his major poetry emerged, and had emphasized the "belated" relation to precursors in the American (Emersonian) Romantic tradition, Shapiro makes a strong case for the value of Ashbery's second book, *The Tennis Court Oath*—especially the long poem "Europe"—as a breakthrough in experimental poetry that problematizes notions of reference through strategies of discontinuity and collage, and he cites *anti*romantic French poetry, modern art, and modern music as powerful influences on his experiments. *John Ashbery: An Introduction to the Poetry* (1979) also includes close readings of the influential long poems, "The Skaters" and "Three Poems," as well as a briefer interpretation of the celebrated "Self-Portrait in a Convex Mirror." Since, in writing the book, he was combatting the frequently articulated view of numerous readers who considered Ashbery's work nonsensical, inchoate, and self-indulgent, Shapiro developed a vigorous, sometimes sarcastic, often poetic counterattack that makes grand claims for this "difficult" poet. In his conclusion, he speaks of "Ashbery's defiant and humorous employment of a fertile formlessness as theme and style." Calling "the darkness in Ashbery . . . rather clear, pointing to the breakdown of causality in contemporary thought and art," Shapiro praises the former's

insight into realms where being in the world seems unfamiliar and self-consuming and the linguistic content peculiarly disordered or hermetic. One of the central functions of an "abstract" poetry is to be aware of itself as non-discursive palpability. Such poetry is involved in particularity without a stable ground. That is the "meaning of meaninglessness," and Ashbery's poignant privacies affirm our elaborated sense of the certainty of uncertainty. (JA, 175)

Since 1979, which was also the year that Jean-François Lyotard's oft-cited *The Postmodern Condition* appeared, the themes of "the breakdown of causality," "particularity without a stable ground," and "the certainty of uncertainty" have become pervasive descriptions, perhaps clichés, of the "groundless ground" of what has come to be known as postmodernist thinking and art. Regrettably, in recent years, the slogans of postmodernism have often served as weak substitutes for careful critical thought about problems of representation and have stood in the way of sufficiently complex interpretations of contemporary cultural products. However, I must caution that Shapiro's critical language in the 1970s, as well as his cogent close readings and his assessments of cultural affiliations and filiations, *did* help many students of poetry develop a cogent sense of Ashbery's contributions. Also, the rhetorical excesses in the Ashbery book can be read chiefly as a polemical response to rigid, conservative scholars and critics. They do not characterize the much more dialectical, rigorous, provisional thinking that one can find in Shapiro's best poetry and in his recent prose. Shapiro's poetry, as I will indicate, has various "postmodernist" characteristics, but it does not cling to the reified version of postmodernist thinking, the automatic rejection of all notions of causal relation and stability, that is currently circulating.

During the year that Shapiro completed his dissertation (1973), his fourth collection of poetry, *The Page-Turner*, appeared. The lyrical "The Night Sky," the jaunty "The Cures of Love," and a few other short poems successfully continue the surreal (and sometimes collagistic) exploration of erotic themes that was more in evidence in *Poems from Deal* than in *A Man Holding an Acoustic Panel*. There are also quicky, engaging poems about family like "A Family Slide" and "Father Knows Best," in which "Father" teaches "the young son" how to "fly" when he "realizes" that the latter "must enclose but a few electrons of air in his fist" (*PT*, 45). One of the few highly disjunctive poems in the book, "Two-Four Time," adroitly combines erotic and family themes. Other memorable poems include the intellectual fantasy, "Life without Mind," and "R's Dilemma," which wittily points to the resistance of dreams to fixed interpretation.

The Page-Turner's most impressive achievement, however, is the nine-page "About This Course," a poem of massive inclusivity—a little like Ashbery's longer "The Skaters," to which it occasionally alludes. In a review in the October 1974 issue of *Poetry*, Jerome J. McGann makes a statement about the entire book that applies more properly to "About This Course": "Fountains, stars, soup, dropping barometers, falling leaves: in Mallarme's sense, these things 'exchange gleams' and 'flame out.' They are the correspondence of and between both listener and sender, reader and writer."[18] The poem begins with a villanelle concerning the description of a "leaf" that "twists and turns, then floats down the drain" (49) and moves on to long-lined, unrhymed, fluid strophes that include several "children's" physics experiments (with adult ramifications about uncertainty), fragmentary scenes of flight and a boat ride, extended biological metaphors, and finally, the illusion of scientific (or erotic?) control:

> We have been sailing in a certain small fountain, like physicists in
>   toy boats
> Each craft bears a candle on its deck. We light the candles and the
>   boats puff by
> As if you were real, delightful. . . .
>   We are fed beside the fountains
> As the young are fed by the experiment and the results.
> It confirms us; and now the whole water is silver.
> A crucial step is taken, but years later,
> The fountain is slowed down, as if controlled by your calm hands.
>   (*PT*, 57)

In "About This Course," we see science utilized, not as the unified answer to all mysteries, the authority above all others, but as a fascinating source for the attempt to construct "the gigantic Lucretian explanatory poem" that does not explain in the usual sense but arrives at "the irresolution of everything." As Shapiro puts it in our unpublished interview: "I love the vocabulary of the natural sciences; I love their unanswerable questions. In physics I love the ecstasy and the incomprehension."

In 1977, Shapiro received the American Academy and Institute of Arts and Letters' Morton Dauwen Zabel Award in Poetry. That year, *Lateness*, his fifth collection, was published. "The Devil's Trill Sonata," a thirty-two page poem, occupies nearly two-thirds of the book. This is one of Shapiro's most powerful achievements, both in a technical and a thematic sense. Divided into three sections, the poem begins with a six-line, then a seven-line strophe, and then the remaining eighty-eight stanzas—with the exception of one tercet—are quatrains, some involving subtle rhymes and off-rhymes. Though lines are generally long, there is a deft modulation between longer and shorter lines that helps make the "Sonata" one of Shapiro's most exquisite musical triumphs.

This is not a poem of one topic or *topos*, but of several, and the frequent deletion of transitions keeps the reader perpetually off balance, never able to impose an overall thematic order on the flow of quatrains. There are elements of erotic poetry, elegy, wild tropes of physical and surreal transformation, direct citations of earlier Shapiro poems, such as "About This Course," joyful and unsatisfactory child's play, other literary and philosophical allusions, a cluster of reimaginings of the Hamlet/Ophelia story, fragments of political protest, parodies of rigid philosophical stances, and "meta-commentary." My fourth chapter will be devoted to a reading of substantial portions of "The Devil's Trill Sonata."

In *Lateness* Harold Bloom aptly finds a powerful "elegiac lyricism" (*L*, back cover).[19] Alluding to the poet's mother, who died in 1975, both the title-poem and the first subpoem in the sequence "Music Written to Order" corroborate Bloom's claim:

> Now and then, now and then, now and then
> Now–ness and then–ness
> And between now and then
> You hear the sound of a projector
> And revisit your ancient home, your new home of late.
> You find only the gardener's sun has survived,
> A detail that wanted to be a Psyche
> Writing daily squibs to the dead.
> A white breast on a white nipple would make a nice sculpture.
> But you would want more milk.
>
> You would want Mother back.
> You go where you must go, Naomi goes
> With Ruth, the record with the record player
> Adults move magnetised to the earth.
> All other insects forage at random. . .
>
> ("Music Written to Order," *L*)

Eschewing sentimentality and biographical data, the poem expresses mourning through delicate gestures and implications. "Between" the opposites, absence/presence, the "projector" (or projection) of mediation and the lack that constitutes longing are "revisited." In the slow rhythm of this "music written to order"—note, of course, the pun either uniting or differentiating the occasional and the metaphysical in the title—they are traced and obliquely named.

In 1980, Shapiro became an assistant professor of Art History at the William Paterson College of New Jersey. Now an associate professor at the college, he has also taught art history and aesthetics at Princeton University and Columbia University. He regularly teaches "Advanced Concepts: Architectural History and Poetry" at Cooper Union, where John Hejduk is dean of architecture. In our 1989 interview, he states:

I have been influenced by my collaborations with the great visionary architect John Hejduk and his penological structures. I'm interested in continuing to work with him on the relations of language and architecture [in book-projects]. I often end this kind of course by suggesting that poetry is always already architecture, and architecture is a structure of meaning. . . . If you've deprived a city of icons and images of meaning, you don't have a city so much as a kind of blank indexical space.

Shapiro's development of an analogy between architecture and poetry, he says, is made "against the idea that poetry is an 'ouch,' an ejaculation, a cry of pain, a shriek of the addresser." For him, "architecture is a refuge, a place of refuge," as well as "a way to suggest that" in poetry, "the first line and the last line are always there." Here, Shapiro is not denying the temporality of the act of reading but insisting that poetry "is a simultaneous structure as much as it is a structure over time" (unpublished interview).

In *To An Idea* (1983), the poet introduces us to a fecund new development in his work, only hinted at fragmentarily earlier. With varying degrees of directness and sustainment, the brilliantly lyrical title-poem, the erotic "An Exercise in Futility," "Commentary Text Commentary Text Commentary Text," "A Spanish Painting," "Mallarmé to Zola," "To the Page," "Thin Snow," and other poems rehearse, disclose, and question various possibilities of representation—whether poetic, philosophical, or artistic. At the same time, these poems consolidate the gains of Shapiro's earlier experimentations. I will save a full discussion of this vital "critical poesis" in Shapiro's work of the 1980s for my second chapter.

To an Idea also includes two powerful poems with overt sociopolitical references, "To the Earth" and "To a Young Exile," in which the threat of nuclear destruction is imagined "beyond this field of books":

They were not thinking we could see anything
But we did see the sentences running over and the

> Two souls you had alas always housed in your breast
> The house loves to be cut up
> Exterior and interior exiles
> I do see and I see also beyond this field of books
> Fangs glistening
> The nations destroyed simultaneously like fireflies
>
> (*TI*, 79)

The theme of sexual desire and imtimacy also figures prominently in the book. Aside from the already mentioned "An Exercise in Futility," two short poems, "The Counter-Example" and "Memory of the Present," and two longer ones, "A Song" and "Valediction Capricien," equal and perhaps surpass the best of Shapiro's earlier erotic poetry with their linguistic inventiveness, tonal variety, and intellectual force. At times, the poems have a lucid simplicity:

> To the mortal beloved
> and to the one of real music
> eyes closed always on the world
> Poor air, I pull you over me to warm this cold night
>
> But what is closure when we are so open
> And what is lack of closure when we are so close.
>
> ("The Counter-Example," *TI*, 23)

Because of its intricate use of repetition and its trenchant investigation of hyperbolic aspects of the rhetoric of love, "A Song"—to be discussed at length in my third chapter—stands as one of Shapiro's most memorable and accomplished erotic poems.

Finally, the long "Friday Night Quartet," divided into a sequence of six subpoems, hauntingly demonstrates Shapiro's mastery of the elegiac mode. Written about the poet's mother but strikingly different from the elegies for her in *Lateness*, the poem refers openly (and frequently in what appears to be her own voice) to specific aspects of her final illness, including the indignities of being treated as a "helpless" patient, humorous and poignant family memories, a fantasy of transcendence through music, and Shapiro's desire to ask his "Mother for a new form / from Paradise" (*TI*, 75). The poem skillfully juxtaposes a great many particular, referential elements without sacrificing the linguistic richness and experimental drive characteristic of the less overtly referential work.

Shapiro's most recent book, *House (Blown Apart)*, includes further explorations of the concerns addressed in *To an Idea*. Many poems lyrically articulate what is "missing," as well as what is viable, in various strategies of representation: "Part of the universe is missing / Sings or says the newspaper, and I believe it. / Even most of it" ("The Lost Golf Ball," 35). Among these poems, the book's title-poem, "A Book of Glass," "A Prayer," "To a Muse," and "Doubting the Doubts" develop the most striking considerations of these issues. The book also contains several luminous erotic poems, such as "December" and "Answers to Odd-Numbered Problems," the latter of which ends with a memorable extinction:

> Efficient as a candle, you stood in those early days
> as if your body was the source, and it was, like a
>   streetlight on a desk.
>
> You were absorbed in your passage through
> this unreasonable mirror. Then scattered by the
>   surface.
> When I look away from you, the room is suddenly
>   extinguished.
>
>   (*HBA*, 39)

Written during Shapiro's disenchantment at the age of Ronald Reagan, *House (Blown Apart)* contains several poems that include a strong measure of social protest. While "The Blank Wall" decries urban decay, "A Fragile Art" speaks pointedly of literal and metaphorical implications of eviction. "A Study of Two Late July Fourths" uses disjunctive collaging to depose empty displays of patriotism:

> Now this little boat in hypnosis sets forth
> It was a collaboration with cardboard bellman and beaver overboard
> Giving up the agony of America or concrete rot
> Like a realist forced to fix the swiftly falling buildings. . . .
>
> Give up capital gain like capital losses

> Capitulate taking it off like a cardigan
> As one who hides a broken Dutchman
> In secret disseizin unlimited misgovernment give up the green
>   helicopter under green trees.
>
> (HBA, 46)

Other noteworthy political poems are the brief, elegant protest "Work in Sadness," and the surreal, satirical "Poem for John Dean."

In 1984, Shapiro's son, Daniel, was born, and several poems in *House (Blown Apart)* celebrate this arrival. In "To a Swan," the celebration occurs in an orgy of anaphora:

> Then you were born, fanatic nut to crack a riddle.
> Then you were born, nude new and dissimilar.
> Then you were born, in a lake like hidden art.
> Then you were born, like a baked sculpture.
> Then you were born, silent repetitive and good.
> Then you were born, swallowing blue-grey and nude. . . .
> Then you were born, out of fanatic architecture and repeating
>   windows
> like art in a lake, like a pill in the rain, as
> an angry swan in the cold dust swallows and rises in the cold
>   wind.
>
> (HBA, 50)

As in Shapiro's other work, sentimentality has no opportunity to prevent the implication of deep feeling from reaching us. A proliferation of tropes breathlessly indicates the inadequacy of language to convey the sublimity of the poet's emotions; nevertheless, the power of the linguistic imagination is affirmed.

Since *House (Blown Apart)*, Shapiro has written two noteworthy sequences of poems, "The Seasons" (named after Jasper Johns's series of paintings) and "After a Lost Original," which is included in a chapbook recently published by Solo Press. Both sequences will appear in the poet's next full length collection. (In chapters two and three respectively, I will discuss two individual poems from "After a Lost Original.") These two sequences are among the poet's most challenging and dynamic work on issues of aesthetic possibility and representation in general.

1
Thresholds of Readability
The Disjunctive Collage-Poems

In *Poets and Painters: Lines of Color,* David Shapiro praises Stephane Mallarmé's bold poetic "project," which "remind[s] us of the distance between signifier and signified, between a name and its object, and between sound and sense in every word. Each word is at once an arbitrary system of music and meaning." Shapiro values Mallarmé's exploitation of linguistic "arbitrariness" not only for its own sake but for its significance as an implicit critique of theories and practices of representation that do not adequately account for the "distances" cited above. Though sometimes appearing to be "an intimist," "at other times, [Mallarmé's] central project seems even nonmimetic or at least drastically antimimetic. . . . The common expectation of sense is again and again deferred so that one begins to presume that nonsense itself is both a topic and a style."[1]

John Ashbery's audacious forays into randomness in *The Tennis Court Oath* (1962)—most notably, "America" and "Europe"—can be seen as an intensification of what Shapiro identifies as Mallarmé's "project." As I have mentioned in the Introduction, Shapiro vigorously defends Ashbery's most disjunctive work from this period in his dissertation and in the revised *John Ashbery: An Introduction to the Poetry.* The younger poet especially values "the successfully *flat* juxtaposition that escapes the merely concrete and demotic . . . and creates a trancelike minimalism . . . what one might call a shorthand and what is now a new *collage-imagism,* concrete dictions, suspended in the colloid of the largely abstract" (*JA,* 60).

Whereas Shapiro holds that the collages of William Carlos Williams in *Paterson* indicate the various elements' "rootedness within a city which is a world" (*JA,* 70), which makes their similarities and differences "meaningful" because of their existence in a "concrete" context, Ashbery's juxtapositions are "flat," because the basis for the relation of elements is absent or nonexistent. Ashbery's "minimalism" deletes worldly contexts and deprives the reader of their reassurance, even as "concrete dictions" are maintained. According to Shapiro, the disorienting "suspension" of this "concreteness" "in the colloid of the largely abstract" constitutes a powerful, nondiscursive representation of the theme of

ontological uncertainty, and this brave use of disjunction seems the most effective vehicle for a poem concerned with large private and public trauma. Like "The Waste Land," its *disjecta membra* is part of a poetically pragmatic presentation of a deformed and abnormal condition. . . . Disjunction, parody, collage, may not necessarily be regressions and anomalies, but a normative response to a culture of commodities. (*JA*, 79)

In writing "Europe," "Ashbery was forced to consider how to unify a composition whose subject was disunity," knowing at the same time that "if unifying intentions become too apparent, the theme of discontinuity is merely artificially presented with a pleasing frame" (*JA*, 72). *Formal (including musical)* aspects are necessary in order to serve as a counterpoint to disjunction, which might otherwise make the poem seem, paradoxically, to be an undifferentiated mass of differences. Shapiro cites Ashbery's "modulation of tone," calling it "dramatic" and often "subtle," and he notes that "structural success" is achieved through the "distribution of the elements of discontinuity so that they are just held in balance, or framed, by the fewest necessary cohesive elements." These "elements," Shapiro continues, "may be *simple tone*, or may be a similar simple *set* of images. . . . While structurally the poems may vacillate, the Proust-like repetition of the elements . . . never rises toward the dangerous omen of a plot but gives *a taste of a plot*" (*JA*, 60–61).

From the mid 1960s to the mid 1970s, David Shapiro followed Ashbery's lead by pursuing experiments with language as a dominantly nonreferential or even *anti*referential medium. In the poems that resulted from these experiments, there is a *collaging* of disparate linguistic elements (from a wide variety of sources) without the writer's supplying a unifying device other than the recurrence of a particular tone or set of images. Neither coherent narrative, nor a definitively identified *persona* or set of characters, nor a clearly operative, overarching thematic context, nor even a linked set of plausible contexts emerges. Although individual phrases, clauses, lines, and occasionally even strophes may "encourage" the reader to assign a literal or figurative meaning, s/he will not be able to supply a meaningful transition between one phrase, clause, line, strophe, or "taste of a plot" and another, even retrospectively. Even when vague suggestions of significance seem to arise, they quickly evaporate.

In one of these disjunctive collage-poems, "The Heavenly Humor," there are recurrent images of "light," the poem's first word (without the "illumination" of a coherent narrative), of music, and of desire. The three images might conceivably be connected—for instance, light and music as emblems of the force of desire—but the poem impedes the possibility of connections through relentless discontinuities, a formal analogue of which is the alternation from extremely long, to medium, to rather short lines:

> Light became audible, that is, a child, and took the empty place.
> Farther back, majesty was a leek to eat. Why make a younger mom
> The thunderbolt of something quick go the round of her lover?
> To themselves, they would guard it,
> Fall upon a ray like the earless. Conquests or a new baby?
> What has happened to Tommy, his violin and bow, must be
>   wedded soon.
> You must strike a beam.
> Since childhood I sat down, sleeve across mouth.
> What cannot be streaked over corpse grey in the land of rectangles.
> Drenches?
> Before the fire? Among airmen, entrusted to slaves,
> I hope the peril in the ice will "experience" him.
> And he was angry, lifted his eyes to the dangers of the mountains.
> My desire sings admirably well but the mail-pilot
> His belt—the toll-gatherer—sometimes does.
> What, they ask, is this science?
>
> (*PD*, 20)

Perhaps line-by-line interpretations of poems like "The Heavenly Humor" could do little but chart the continually reiterated movement between a reader's desperate attempt to latch onto a context and the poem's speedy disruption of that contextual possibility. The reader experiences continual "perturbation" and is unable to tell whether there are supposed to be many "voices" in a poem like "The Heavenly Humor" or one speaking subject "inhabited" by many "voices" that s/he has internalized or imagined. Also, where does one "voice" leave off and another begin, as in the strange sentence, "Why make a younger mom / The thunderbolt of something quick go the round of her lover?" which is split in several places by syntactical anomalies.

If we take the notion of "readability" as the translation of the words of a poem into a coherent narrative or thematically unified articulation, then Shapiro's disjunctive collage-poems are perhaps unreadable. (Of course, what is to stop an interpreter from arbitrarily assigning a dramatic context and ignoring whatever textual details do not fit within it? While some radical relativists would argue that, in the process of interpretation, all texts are used as a pre-text for developing a fiction, I would counter that it would be much harder to do this persuasively with a disjunctive collage-poem by Shapiro or Ashbery than with most other texts.) However, if we decide to accept "perturbation" as a norm and to respect the poems' heterogeneity and not to demand from them what the author evidently does not wish them to give, can such poems at least be considered readable on their own terms?

On the one hand, a reader can adopt the general principle that s/he will not demand thematic unity or a narrow "distance between signifier and signified" from a poem; on the other hand, individual parts of the poem seem "readable" in a traditional sense and hence allow for the possibility in the reader's mind that overall referential coherence might eventually emerge, despite temporary disjunctions. For example, in the opening line of "The Heavenly Humor," one can easily suppose that the synesthesia is representing the vision of a child giving way to the audition of his/her voice, and in that process, the child taking an "empty place," whether physical or psychological. The reader might think that, in the course of the poem, there will be a representation of something happening to the child or to the viewer/auditor in relation to him/her. However, such an expectation is squashed—again and again. When there are references to "Tommy," apparently a child, and "childhood," and similar references in a later part of the poem, which I have not quoted, none of these develop the hint of a theme in the first line. Another referential "tease" involves a situation in which there seems to be a statement in the poem that refers to what is going on in it, as in the line, "They're all mad, leading me into the inappropriate feeling range," in "The Heavenly Humor." This line can be construed as a commentary by one "voice" on the madness and maddening impact of all the other "voices." However, no subsequent part of the poem supports this interpretation.

I am suggesting, then, that, despite sincere intentions to give up the "hunt" for referentiality, a reader will have immense difficulty not being "seduced" occasionally to resume the hunt—"seduced" by the notion that signifiers seem at times to be pointing strongly at determinate signifieds. Language can sometimes approach the abstract condition of wordless music or the abstract materiality of paint in—let us say—abstract-expressionist art of the 1950s, but it does not go the whole distance. Hence, even if the reader senses that a poem should not be read for referential "content," s/he will probably do so at points in the reading process and then be "slapped" by an antimimetic movement in the poem. While the text never emerges as "readable" in a traditional sense, it is always hovering near the threshold of readability.

Shapiro notes in the "Prolegomenon" to his book on Ashbery that "there is an icy autocratic humiliation of the reader, who expects again and again a center, only to be decentered" (*JA*, 1). However, in the course of reading a poem like "Europe" or "The Heavenly Humor," when expectations of referential certainty are thwarted, perhaps the reader can learn to find his/her textual frustration a source of fascination or humor and thus reduce the level of frustration. In Henri Bergson's *Laughter*, an audience is said to laugh at the revelation of a character's inelasticity. In this case, the reader as audience can see an aspect of him/herself as an inelastic character, while a particular movement of the poem brings out that laughable rigidity on the "stage" of reading. Liberated temporarily from the quest for determinate meaning by playful self-mockery, the reader can allow him/herself to experience and enjoy the poem's "music" (rhythm, off-rhymes, assonance, alliteration, dissonance, etc.) apart from any relation to sense.

It would be cumbersome to write (or read) a thorough representation of the kind of reading process that I am characterizing in a general way, but I can at least give a "taste" of one. This passage from the beginning of the title poem of *Poems from Deal* is a typical example of the slippery territory of Shapiro's highly disjunctive collage-poems:

1.
How wonderful to be in the arms of cerebral creatures.
You taste garage, moon, strength.
You have only a live child and fresh water on your arms.

2.
You take back. The hot shower drum roll.
 In that echo chamber, musicians have
showered. Evenings they swing up the vulture's
beak. But you fight with your teeth,
resuscitating few beaks. Why not fight me
in the Venus flower way. I'm happy for the anger
 you showed your room. Hating shining hating.

(*PD*, 24)

The first line expresses a straightforward erotic enthusiasm, and the reader might expect that a "report," whether direct or indirect, about a sensual experience will follow. However, a "you" is told in the second line that s/he tastes three "things" that do not seem to go together at all and do not seem connected to someone being "in the arms of cerebral creatures." What convoluted cerebration is taking place? How can one "taste garage," when it is ridiculous enough to "taste garbage"? Perhaps the connection of "moon" to the wholly abstract noun, "strength," can be justified as a romantic metonymy, but what does "moon" have to do with "garage" or "garage" have to do with "strength"? If "you" might be "in the arms of cerebral creatures" and "tasting" these disparate "things," then how is it that "a live child and fresh water" are "on your arms"? What context can possibly enclose these weird assertions or deracinated bits of narration? The title is no help; it merely announces that the "poems" are "from" a town in New Jersey named Deal, where, in fact, the poet lived at an early point in his life. The reader may laugh at his/her own hopeless demand that a set of juxtapositions that so wildly refuses ordinary sense conform to expectations.

The opening sentence of section two makes no conventional

sense, because this is the kind of sentence that requires an object to complete the thought, and it lacks one. But does this matter? Musically, it is a kind of punctuation, coming after a long sentence, a medium-sized one, and an even longer one in the three-lined first section. Appropriately, this anomalous sentence is followed by a strange fragment: perhaps a "hot shower" may sound like a "drum roll," and could it possibly refer back to the "fresh water on your arms"? If the reader is now tempted—by this possibility, by the sense that the shower stall is a kind of "echo chamber," and by the sudden information that "musicians have / showered"—to resume the comically collapsed hunt for coherent meaning, s/he is almost immediately thrown off the trail by the notion that the "musicians"—if "they" refers to them—are brought into inexplicable contact with the previously unmentioned "vulture's / beak."

The "you"—possibly the same one who had been tasting the bizarre assortment, having "a live child," and "fresh water"—is reintroduced as one who fights with absurd "weapons": "teeth." Also, this "you" is unable to resuscitate, not the "vultures," but their "beaks." Each successive detail takes the reader farther and farther from a recognizable context, until s/he laughs again at this fresh attempt to impose one. Now a speaker—for how can we assume that it is the same "voice" who spoke the previous line—introduces the fighter to "fight me / in the Venus flower way." "The Venus flower" could be a trope of love, or of the "Venus fly trap," but at this point, the reader may realize that it will not help to think that s/he can figure out which one (if either) is intended. The strophe closes with a commendation to the addressee "for the anger / you showed your room" (not *in* the room or shower or echo chamber, as though the room would appreciate the sharing of feelings) and a fragment allowing the anger or something similar to it ("hating") to sandwich another gerund, "shining." When the quest for meaning has fallen apart again, one may review the strophe and notice that the medial caesuras in the lines of this strophe—as opposed to the end-stopped lines of the previous section—produce a choppy, fragmented effect, like the reading experience of trying to focus on one bit of narrative or lyric information and having it violently displaced by the next. Sound does not exactly echo sense, but the loss of sense.

I have singled out Shapiro's highly disjunctive collage-poems as the most extreme experiments of the poems collected in *Poems from Deal*, *A Man Holding an Acoustic Panel*, and *The Page-Turner*—and one or two, in fact, also appear in *Lateness* and *To an Idea* respectively. However, it should be noted that these poems comprise a relatively small portion of the work in these volumes, even though, as the poet has told me, he wrote hundreds of pages of poetry in that vein in the 1960s, and, at the age of seventeen, tried to formulate a theory of poetic discontinuity. (One can easily imagine the young Shapiro wishing to publish a greater quantity of his highly disjunctive work and being told forcefully by editors that more accessible poems would prove more palatable to readers.)

From his most extreme experiments, Shapiro obviously learned a great deal about precise ways in which reference is thwarted or displaced, and this knowledge helped him a great deal in developing the poetry in which elements displaying various degrees of referential determinacy interact with elements of dominant nonreferentiality. This more inclusive collage-poetry—most in evidence in Shapiro's last book of the 1970s, *Lateness*, and his first of the 1980s, *To an Idea*—is susceptible to the reader's imposition or discovery of relatively large blocks of narrative or thematic coherence, but, in important ways, resists the elucidation of an overall context by erupting at various points in antimimetic, decontextualizing ways. These poems make enough use of disjunctive strategies to foreground the practical study of the "arbitrariness" and "music" of language and the "deferral" of "the common expectation of sense." A powerful example of poetry in this mode is "Commentary Text Commentary Text Commentary Text," whose triply emphatic title belies the fact that the poem contains a great deal of surrealistic, unstable descriptive language and only a few fragments of abstraction that gesture in the direction of commentary. The poem begins:

> In the morning, the water fed the sky,
> Eyes of another material had been inserted and the hair,
>   gathered into high strands, more carefully arranged.
> Two more bodies were discovered in the Spanish
> forest fire.
> Sky like sand, sand like a body

Sun like a breast one faintly outlined

In blue magic marker and bleeding into the margin
Of its own sunny space.

(TI, 24)

The surreal reversal of the first line provides an immediate stumbling block to meaning-seekers: Perhaps an ocean wave or geyser has leaped high, as though to the heavens, but what is the feeding all about? Does the sky require "breakfast" because it is a trope for some living being? In reading the second line, one might surmise that the poet is describing a surrealist's or a child's collage-painting, which contains a landscape that possesses features of a human head, including "eyes of another material" that "had been inserted" and not painted, and "the hair, / gathered into high *strands*"—the pun emphasizing the double sense of human and natural imagery.

But then, perhaps to indicate that the reader cannot be so sure that a collage-painting or drawing has just been described, a sentence from a decidedly alien context intrudes grimly. It is a realistic-seeming "news item," the discovery of bodies in the "landscape" of a forest (fire). At once, this apparent realism is disrupted by a parade of similes linking "sky," "sand," and "body" and "sun" and "breast," indicating, like Mallarmé's notion of correspondences, the endless and dizzying possibilities of the substitution of one sign for another in the poetic and painterly imagination. The material quality of the artistic medium, however, signified by the "blue magic marker . . . bleeding into the margin" of the sun's "own sunny space," stresses the establishment of difference more than the unifying aspect of metaphor. When margins are violated, it leads to a contamination of one element by another and marks their agitated inherence within one another's "space"—without coalescence or a coherent stasis.

Without any warning, the poem articulates a relationship between speaker and addressee and moves to the theme of negation:

And a stable bridge linking us no longer
August like autumn and the new encyclopedia
Nom de guerre: Nothing.

> Nonobservance, nonappearance, noncompletion.
>
> Like the bright male cardinal on the red maple.
>
> (TI, 24)

Already, Shapiro has constructed several unstable linguistic bridges in this poetic landscape, and so the first line of the passage above is an appropriate description of the "breaching" of the usual "contract" of determinate meaning between author and reader that I have been discussing in the course of this chapter. Given the erotic dimension of the comparison of sun and breast in the previous lines, however, it might also refer to the sundering of a love relationship, and this possibility seems to be confirmed later, in the last three lines of the poem. In the meantime, after the positioning of an extremely shaky bridge on the basis of weak alliteration and temporal contiguity ("August like autumn") and a quizzical mention of "the new encyclopedia" (a sign of the attempted gathering of immense and diversive knowledge, but placed inside a poem whose disruptive collage-form seems to question the kind of closure implicitly promised by such a gathering), there is a catalog of negations, underscored by two uses of single-line strophes and the resulting emphasis of white spaces.

Generally, an alias or *"Nom de guerre"* helps an individual deflect attention from his/her inherited social identity in order to gain a measure of freedom in constructing a new one, but the name of "nothing" subverts individuality altogether. Shapiro's procession of "non" words on a single line is especially interesting: "nonobservance" may signify the breaking of ritual or law, as well as a simple failure to see, whereas "nonappearance" suggests the absence of a physical manifestation, and "noncompletion" states the failure of a process to reach its goal. Prompted by the line's tripartite structure, which repeats the structure of the poem's title, I am tempted to read the procession as a self-referential "commentary" on the refusal of this particular art work to "observe," make present, and "complete" the "rituals" of certain formal and rhetorical traditions for the representation of landscape and for mimesis in general. On the other hand, if the line refers to a love relationship, there is a "nonobservance" of the rites of love, a "nonappearance" of the lovers to each other, and a "noncompletion" of the aims of love. As for "the bright male cardinal on the red maple"—red on red—this living element of a landscape may be ensconced in "nonappearance," because the figure/ground distinction seems to have collapsed, as in many minimalist and color-field paintings. The poem concludes with a six-line strophe that musically juxtaposes long and short lines:

> No man's land and no mistake. No wonder.
> Noah's ark nocturne.
> Inferno black Purgatorio matte gray Paradise is almost white
> *Present I flee you*
> *Absent I have you*
> Your name like landscape written across the middle of the page.
> (*TI*, 24)

Is the poet naming the kind of "landscape" devised in the first part of the poem—whether by an imagined visual artist or a child at play or simply through his own linguistic imagination—"no man's land"? A self-referential reading of this continuation of the drift of negation fits well: the disjunctive effects of collage, coupled with a stream of similes ("sky like sand, sand like a body," etc.), does not permit any interpreter to identify the boundaries of a determinate territory and thus, in a sense, lay claim to it. Also, the undermining of territorial claims is "no mistake" on the writer's part. The fragment, "no wonder," humorously supports this notion: the poet thwarts the desire for interpretive decisiveness by giving no "map" for readers to determine whether the words are to be read as the usual cliché ("of course" this is true) or as an assertion or lament that there is no *sense* of wonder, perhaps in the reception of the landscape. Once again, however, the three negations might be referring to the loss of the "possession" of love (or the idea that love has never actually been "possessed"), the intentional severing of a relationship by the beloved, and either the inevitability of the severing or the lamentable loss of "wonder" (enthusiasm) in the speaker's experience following the negation of love.

Next, an off-rhyme with the "nos" of the previous line links the problematic space of landscape (or of a love relationship) with a music of destruction: that of Noah's ark during the night of the nearly all-negating flood. Jumping from the Old Testament to

Dante's *Divine Comedy*, Shapiro pretends to find a color scheme to fit the three "landscapes" of the after-life. Interestingly, "Paradise"—like Robert Rauschenberg's, Jasper Johns's, and Robert Ryman's so-called "white" paintings—"is almost white," since white may be considered an absolute, beyond attainment in the material world, and since no form of depiction can capture the absoluteness of heavenly bliss.

While the speaker had posited an "us" in the middle of the poem, possibly alluding to the "interaction" between an artist and a landscape, or the transaction between a writer and a reader, or a love relationship, his concluding three lines poignantly address a "you." "Present" (but to what or whom?), the "I" dashes to absence from the other, whereas, when "absent" (from the other), he feels in possession (presence) of the other. Since each element of the binary pair calls its opposite, the oscillation creates a sense of "noncompletion" and "no man's land." Does the poet or artist beholding a landscape somehow "flee" the task of representing it and yet possess a trace of the depiction of landscape through an awareness of its absence, through articulation of obstacles in the path of reference? Does the reader's attention to the poem, in signifying his/her proximity to the poem, indicate the "flight" of the poet and of the unproblematic reception of his poetic intentions, or does the poet utilize his absence to lure the reader into being "possessed" by the difficulties of the poem as s/he reads? Does the physical presence of the beloved make the lover flee when he realizes that "possession" of or unification with her is impossible, and does her physical absence impel him to create a fiction of his possession of her—a fiction that he takes, sometimes, as fact?

Notice that the poem's last line does not compare the other (whether natural scene, reader, or lover) to a landscape but presents "your *name* like landscape written across the middle of the page." "Name," of course, may or may not be taken literally. A landscape painting is, however close or far to conventions of realism, a sign (name) for the landscape that fills space as an actual landscape does, though confined to the mere "middle" of a canvas or page. The reader can be considered a re-writer whose interpretation of a poetic text acts as his/her sign of author-ity or assumption of space ("like landscape"), the signature metaphorically displacing the "original" poet's, as though "written across the middle of the page." Finally, while the beloved is physically absent from the speaker, the latter "has" her in the sense that he makes a sign of her absence, not literally but figuratively her "name," the presence that fills the page "like landscape."

In poems like "Commentary Text Commentary Text Commentary Text," not only does the collaging of disparate elements—detached from their divergent contexts—disrupt coherent commentary and allow various fragments to disrupt and "perturb" each other, but the ambiguous uses of particular abstractions and concrete images, as well as pronouns without determinate antecedents, allow the interpreter to develop multiple, fragile, but intriguing conjectures about overall context that neither support nor quite annihilate each other. In my account of "Commentary Text Commentary Text Commentary Text," I find that more "commentary" has been *produced* than I could muster for highly disjunctive collage-poems like "The Heavenly Humor." But a troubling question remains: Have I arrived at a threshold of reading, am I forced to pause there, or have I crossed it?

2
Desire, Representation, and Critique

In Wallace Stevens's long poem, "The Man with the Blue Guitar," we find the claim: "Poetry is the subject of the poem, / From this the poem issues and / / To this returns,"[1] and in another, later long poem, "An Ordinary Evening in New Haven," the speaker states that "This endlessly elaborating poem / Displays the theory of poetry, / As the life of poetry."[2] Although these assertions may appear to support an argument in favor of "art for art's sake" and against the attempt to relate art to the social world, they can be given a much different interpretation. "Poetry" here does not have to be construed in a narrow sense, but as the effort to discover what various attempts at representation—including poetry—can and should accomplish and what they should not attempt and cannot achieve.

Like the Stevens of "The Man with the Blue Guitar," "Notes Toward a Supreme Fiction," and "An Ordinary Evening in New Haven," a sizeable number of twentieth-century American poets with a wide variety of aesthetic and sociopolitical orientations include an explicit investigation and/or critique of notions of representation in some of their poems. These include the "high modernist" T. S. Eliot in *Four Quartets*, the former "Imagist" William Carlos Williams in *Paterson*, and Charles Olson in *The Maximus Poems*. Among living poets, Robert Creeley, Adrienne Rich, John Ashbery (as Shapiro and various others demonstrate in readings of "Self-Portrait in a Convex Mirror"), A. R. Ammons, and younger writers like Ishmael Reed, Margaret Atwood, Audre Lord, David Lehman, Ann Lauterbach, and the so-called "Language Poets" like Charles Bernstein, Ron Silliman, and Susan Howe can be cited.

Why have so many modern and contemporary poets taken up "the theory of poetry" (in a general sense) in their poetry itself?

To gesture toward a complex situation in an overly schematic fashion (for the sake of brevity), there have been widespread conflicts in the twentieth century between those who continue to affirm what may be perceived as the encrustations of received "knowledge" (that announces its fixity, universality, and absolute coherence) and those who articulate the notion that there are no absolute "centers" that govern metaphysics, theology, science, and the arts, and that provide an unquestionable point of departure for further work. Numerous critics, among them David Shapiro, have founded their descriptions and evaluations of the work of literary authors, artists, and speculative thinkers on some version of this distinction. For example, Jean-Francois Lyotard in his influential *The Postmodern Condition,* cited in my Introduction, has declared that the opposition of the second group to the tenets of the first comprises the most salient feature of "postmodern" thinking. For those sharing or leaning toward a postmodern "stance," the purposes of writing poetry or making art must be reconsidered and rearticulated, and the art form itself is a "logical" place for that rethinking to occur.

Of all the poets mentioned earlier, I believe that Wallace Stevens has been most influential in David Shapiro's explicit investigations of the general problem of representation in numerous poems written in the 1980s, after *Lateness.* Whereas John Ashbery's poems in this vein tend to move quickly from a consideration of an aspect of representation to another theme or a thematic collapse, Stevens's—like Shapiro's—often sustain the exploration for at least the "average" length of a lyric poem (or the size of one of Stevens's "cantos" in his long, meditative poems).

While various critics argue that Stevens—in "modernist" rather than "postmodernist" fashion—actually desires and quests for the *experience* of a unified, "centered," totalized awareness in the form of a "supreme fiction," which can only be temporary, Paul A. Bové counters that Stevens "actively employs the *telos*-oriented quest metaphor against itself not merely to show that there is no center but to test in fiction various poetic and personal myths and metaphors in a world with no firm point of reference." According to Bové, Stevens consciously writes "fictions" to perform "tests" of "received and acquired 'truths'" so that he may "destroy their hardened existence, to discard what is now useless and obscuring, and to release what had long ago disclosed itself and become the origin of the particular myth or metaphor."[3]

I would question the Heideggerian rhetoric of the "disclosure" of mythological "origins"; perhaps this can be taken, more adequately, to mean that Stevens pursued the desire behind the quest for fictions at the same time as he "destroyed" the fictions' "hardened existence." Otherwise, while Bové's formulation can underwrite extremely persuasive readings of Stevens's texts, I do not know precisely how one could determine whether this view of Stevens's attitude about received fictions in his poetry or the "nostalgic" view cited earlier has a greater claim to accuracy, or whether the poet's work is the site of a complex ambivalence. Nevertheless, Bove's characterization lucidly traces the "point of departure" for Shapiro's poetic explorations of the problems of representation, as my close readings of three poems will now indicate.

In a treatment of issues of representation—whether in the work of poets like Stevens and Shapiro or of philosophers like Derrida and Foucault or of artists like Jasper Johns—questions of origin and originality play a significant role. The consideration of the "supreme fiction" of absolute originality in Stevens's poetry is often linked with the idea of unmediated perception, and this linkage reemerges for scrutiny in the title-poem of Shapiro's *To an Idea*. Of course, even though the poem's title has an indefinite article (rather than the supreme "the"), it recalls the Platonic *eidos*—pure idea, beyond sensory experience (*meta*-physical) that Stevens reworks into the more sensory orientation of "the first idea."

In the first canto of "Notes toward a Supreme Fiction," Stevens proclaims to his "ephebe":

Begin, ephebe, by perceiving the idea
Of this invention, this invented world,
The inconceivable idea of the sun.

You must become an ignorant man again
And see the sun again with an ignorant eye
And see it clearly in the idea of it.[4]

Ringing with the Cartesian desire for clarity, this noble "ignorance" involves stripping away all names, all myths, all images, and metaphors for the sun. One must somehow move beyond the constraints of language: "Phoebus was / A name for something that never could be named." And yet, even as he speaks of going "beyond" or "above" names, Stevens adds a name in an apposition: "The sun / Must bear no name, gold flourisher, but be / In the difficulty of what it is to be."[5] In poetry, of course, the attempt to gesture "beyond" language is performed in language, which permits space for "what it is to be" only through "names."

Nevertheless, Stevens's speaker considers it an essential, ineradicable desire to quest for unmediated perception. Its realization is to be *imagined* temporarily. Thus, the glimpsing of "the first idea" is a "supreme fiction" that provides a fundamental consolation amid frustration and daily boredom:

> The poem refreshes life so that we share,
> For a moment, the first idea. . . . It satisfies
> Belief in an immaculate beginning
>
> And sends us, winged by an unconscious will,
> To an immaculate end.[6]

In the opening lines of "To an Idea," Shapiro's speaker lucidly rearticulates the desire for "an immaculate beginning," a genesis without antecedent, but he does so *in the past tense*—thus creating some distance between himself and the desire—and paradoxically:

> I wanted to start *Ex Nihilo*
> I mean as a review of sorts.
> It's too much of a burst for some,
> Too unanalyzably simple for others,
> As one called perspective that vicious
> Doctrine, but is it: to know nothing,
> To taste something, dazzled by absence,
> By your chair, by the chair of Salome?
>
> (*TI*, 15)

Given the echoes of Plato, Stevens, and others in the title itself, Shapiro's speaker is "reviewing" the history of the desire for original, unmediated perception and of attempts to fulfill it; he is not perpetuating the desire ahistorically. A pun in the second line underscores the notion that the closest the speaker could have come to starting *Ex Nihilo* was not very close: "a review of *sorts*"—not only "a sort of review" but a review of different *ways* of attempting the impossible project.

While the violence ("burst") of such a reimagining is too much "for some," others find it reductive, hence inimical to analytic elaboration. Half a millenium ago, "perspective" probably seemed astonishingly *"Ex Nihilo"* and "vicious" in its severe reduction of the complexities of visual representation of three-dimensionality into a rather rigid formula. Echoing Socrates ("but is it: to know nothing") and yet swerving away from the quest for "pure idea" with an acknowledgment of the material world ("To taste something"), Shapiro's speaker questions whether the quest to wipe the slate clean is really too disorienting or too simple. If Stevens's speaker in the lines from "Notes" cited earlier focuses on the plenitude of the imagination's temporary accomplishment of its "supreme fiction," whereas, in "The Snow Man," the wintry quest for the first idea is reduced to the austerity of "nothing," Shapiro permits a concentration on the *"Nihilo"* (nothing) as much as on the movement out of it *("ex")*, the notion of being "dazzled by absence," as Freud was dazzled by the empty chair reserved for his beloved Salome at a lecture he gave.

In the second half of the poem, the speaker performs a series of dedications. Like Frank O'Hara's notion of "Personism," in which "the poem is at last between two persons instead of two pages,"[7] his structure of address (a kind of apostrophe) constitutes a material presence (the literary work) that tenuously articulates a bridging of distance between two "absences," the artistic creator and the object of the dedication:

Or yet another familiar dedication:
To an idea, writ in water,
To wild flesh, on the surface alone,
To you who carried me like mail
From one house to another.
Now the cars go past the lake, as if copying could exist.
The signs shine, through the Venetian blinds.

(15)

With its Spenserian tone, "an idea, writ in water" underscores the fascination of mutability. It also evokes the section of Stevens's "Notes" entitled "It [the Supreme Fiction] Must Change," in which "a will to change" is "too constant to be denied, // The eye of a vagabond in metaphor / That catches our own."[8] "Wild flesh" itself can be read as a trope of mutability, and its "surface" status marks it as an "idea" divorced from the usual layers of allegorical significance.

The third and last dedication seems to "perturb" us, to throw us off-track, and thus to enact the movement of absence traced earlier. Made to a direct addressee, a partly unidentified "you," this dedication makes the poem's speaker into an object or a transported signifier or text ("like mail"). Is the poet's mother carrying him *ex nihilo* from the "house" of nonbeing to that of being? Are his parents literally bringing him as an infant from one dwelling place to another? Is the poem carrying him from an "idea" to the reader, or is a beloved transporting him from one emotional state to another? Is the "me" to be considered a sign for the poem itself being carried from the mind of the poet to the mind of the reader, or is the dedication made to the idea of transition itself?

Next, the speaker jumps from a dedication based on a past recollection to an apparent present involving the particularized image of the cars' movement. Probably, the moving cars have been imperfectly and fleetingly reflected in water, itself in transit, though the cars might be seen as a trope (failed "copy") of their drivers' erotic desires. The speaker reviews the "idea" of representation, "writ in water"—that distorting mirror—and finds that it cannot be brought to full presence any more than the "first idea" of *ex nihilo* creation cited at the poem's beginning. The preposition in the dedication, "*to* an idea," may mark an unbridgeable distance, a continual deferral of arrival, as in Ashbery's poem "As You Came from the Holy Land," which concludes bleakly with "emptiness . . . distributed / in the idea of what time it is / when that time is already past."[9]

In the last image of "To an Idea," the speaker is not so much "dazzled by absence" as by mediations, the spacings that comprise a complex play of absence and presence. One is dazzled by the fragmentary perceptions caused by arbitrary and shifting contexts of representation: "The signs shine, through the Venetian blinds." If the adjective "Venetian" suggests desire, this erotic impulse may have a partially "blinding" and partially eye-opening effect. These blinds are both a barrier to seeing and a set of frames sometimes permitting external representations (*not* essences or "pure ideas") to "shine" into one's dwelling place. While, toward the beginning of "Notes," Stevens's speaker calls for unmediated perception of the sun, Shapiro creates a lyric closure (by no means an image of transcendence) out of the highly mediated perception of signs, which may include sunlight. The implications of layering and of the co-existence of illumination and shadow in the closure of "To an Idea" remind me of the effects of layering in Jasper Johns's drawings. As Shapiro notes in his study of the drawings, the artist "ruptures space and line because he wants to underline the notion that unity is merely notational. . . . Drawing is both the caressing of the icon and its deletion under a cloud of doubts. . . . Johns opens and closes boundaries with ruptures."[10]

In "To an Idea," as in much of Johns's art, the poet quickly debunks the notion that he can arrive at a point of *original* perception—either in the sense that he can "see" all the way back to a theological, metaphysical, or aesthetic "origin" through his "reading" of culture or in the sense that he can perceive a phenomenological present "Truth" that no one else has seen or can see. From this awareness, Shapiro indicates that one is neither reduced to nostalgic longing (although he admits that "absences" can be "dazzling") nor frozen in the passive acceptance of surface and of imminent experience: A perceiver can *read* palimpsests, which do not disclose an absolute "Truth" on the basis of accretion or any other principle, but allow one to perceive the interaction of different layers of representation in history as an ongoing process of disclosures and concealments.

In the recent poem, "After a Lost Original," the first poem in a sequence of that name, Shapiro explores issues of origin and originality in a strikingly different way than in "To an Idea." In place of a particularized supreme fiction of origin, Shapiro weaves a fiction of unpredictable and disorienting shifts:

When the translation and the original meet
The doubtful original and the strong mistranslation
The original feels lost like a triple pun
And the translation cries, Without me you are lost

> Then be my dream, thin as the definition
> Of a trance in a garden
> The ambiguous friend responds, Perhaps I do astonish you
> Like a boy confused with a butterfly's dream.[11]

The possibility of triple meaning in the first word of Shapiro's title ("After") introduces the problem that the operations of language pose for the project of recuperating origins. According to a literary convention of titles, one is not translating (literally, in the Latin derivation, "bringing [something] across") but writing in the "spirit" of an original, *or*, to cite a more colloquial meaning, one is in pursuit of the original, *or*, to cite the most common use, one is marking one's temporal relationship to it. Not only is "after" a shifty word, but the poem proceeds to indicate that both "lost" and "original" are equally difficult to pin down.

As it represents the "meeting" of the "original" and the "translation," Shapiro's poetic language is full of puns and qualifications, raising questions in the reader's mind about whether the former really can be what its name indicates it is. In other words, while the "original" came into being earlier in time than the "translation" did, is it something that really originates—that is, constitutes the kind of *ex nihilo* creation mentioned at the beginning of "To an Idea"—or did something or some concept as yet unidentified give it form or substance? Personified, the original is "full of doubt," perhaps about the status implied in its name. The original named in the poem may be a text or a "first idea" or "supreme fiction" of absolute originality, or it may be something or someone invested with parental status, just as the "translation" may be assigned a child's position. Whatever they "are"—and readers can only guess—both "translation" and "original" are textualized: they are tropes in a poem. While the translation is usually supposed to represent or stand in place of the original, because some readers find the latter indecipherable, in the poem they are both present and interact with one another, like the pages of a bilingual edition or a parent and child. But why is the "translation" refigured as a "strong mistranslation"? Perhaps the poet intends to say that a translation, no matter how scrupulous, can never fully translate. At best, because of the fact that language always has the potential to break away from finite relationships between signifier and signified (or between a signifier in one "language" and a signifier in another), the translation can always open up different possibilities of reading from the original. Analogously, a child may repeat the genetic code of the two parents but "mistranslates" the parents by developing particular traits that do not replicate those of either parent.

Since the possibility of polysemy, including punning, is intrinsic to the material properties of words, "naturally," the untranslatable "original feels lost like a triple pun" when faced by "the strong mistranslation." Any signifier in the former might be assigned three or more meanings, dependent on its inclusion in or exclusion from various possible contexts. The word "lost" itself may suggest that the original's distance from the copy, its (personified) sense of vexation, or its absence from the supreme fiction of originality.

If originals are generally accorded a higher value than translations, the personified translation performs what one might call a deconstructive overturning or reversal[12] of the hierarchy of that binary opposition by reminding the original: "Without me you are lost." Although, the translation mistranslates, it does carry across a trace of what has been lost, which its "predecessor" cannot do for itself—in the sense that it is otherwise indecipherable to particular readers. From this perspective, the translation *makes* the original seem original by helping to assign it a readable position at a specific point in history. Similarly, after parents are dead, the child can be said to carry a "trace" of them through the perpetuation of a name, memory, and genetic imprints. Thus, the parents depend on the child to "translate" them into a "life"–in–death.

In this little drama, the original is granted a living voice and expresses the desire to reclaim priority by making the translation its "dream, thin as the definition / Of a trance in a garden." The translation, however, refuses to be considered "thin": its *thickness* involves its words' material specificity, differing from the precursor's words, just as the child's physical and psychological and historical specificity thickly differs from the parents' characteristics. One who *trans*lates is not necessarily en*tranc*ed by the original but engaged in the act of creating a new text that stands in relation to the old one. Thus, the translation has a degree of "originality" and cannot be accurately viewed as the product of what it is translating. Just as the parents cannot reduce the child to an agent for the fulfilment of their desires, since the child has differing desires of his/her own, the scriptive translation's differences from the original can be said to "astonish" and "confuse" the latter, as in the bizarre collision of "boy" and "butterfly's dream."

In the second half of the poem, the translation first maintains and elaborates on its reversal of the traditional hierarchy, and then the narrator exposes further problems in the way the binary opposition operates:

But you are my dream now, after all
If I don't think of you, you disappear
Like a slice through two trees for a thousand years
Return knowing coldly a need for guerdons, guardians
Letters written on clouds, snakes on curtains and naked devices
Frighten them no longer since they live only together
Refracted through blue green black moss
They travel together to the margins of a cloud.

In its response, the translation rearticulates its power over the original "now"—at this moment in history—when the latter is absent from people's consciousness and *needs* the former to "dream" it in order for it to "exist" as a text to be read. The possible thousand-year "disappearance" of the original, itself a dream of negation, is compared to the simultaneously violent and yet tonally understated image of "a slice through two trees"—performed, let us say, by a gigantic and remarkably powerful electric saw! Indeed, all texts are subject to the possibility of oblivion, the chance that readers will not read them, perhaps "for a thousand years." This indicates that whatever "laws" of representation a philosopher, linguist, or poet may "discover" do not transcend the unpredictable, historical processes of the construction, appropriation, dissemination, loss, and discarding of texts, which significantly affect the possible deployments and disappearance of modes of representation.

One can also read these lines as a child, assuming a solipsistic stance, insisting to a parent that the latter only exists as a representation in the offspring's mind. This "selfish" stance does not necessarily reflect a fully held belief but may involve an exaggerated representation of the child's desire to assert his/her autonomy against the parent's greater social power. Then again, this makes more "logical" sense if the child is speaking of a future in which the parent is deceased and thus can literally be considered a "dream" or memory by the living offspring. (Of course, in such a case, the child is forgetting what I noted earlier about the "translation" of the genetic code.)

After dreaming of the original's disappearance, the translation tells the original that it is allowed to return with a (newly acquired?) appreciation of the need to be validated and protected from the forces of disappearance ("guerdons, guardians"). The virtuosity of the near-rhyme may suggest that these two benefits can be produced partly through attention to linguistic play. Having completed their dialogue, the narrator declares that original and translation are now unafraid of various ominous signs—including "letters written on clouds" (either epistolary communications or single characters) and "snakes on curtains"—"since they live only together."

Given the fantasy that the personified texts can talk to each other in the poem, this last assertion is not surprising: They "live together" as words or "characters" in the linguistic or dramatic "house" of "After a Lost Original," as a "literal" original and translation would "live" facing each other in a bilingual edition. Nevertheless, as a meditation on representation which has provided hints about the likely impossibility of absolute translation, the poem invites the reader to question this assertion from another standpoint. The physical copresence of original and translation is a possibility, but the phrase, "they live only together," can also be interpreted as a sign of a powerful (and powerfully questionable) *metaphysical* "dream": the notion that one who knows both languages can ensure that the latter is "faithful" to the *intention* "embodied" by the former, that the latter is as close as possible to a "translation" rather than a "mistranslation."

In his use of language in the last two lines of the poem, as in earlier tropes, Shapiro points to the hopelessness of this dream. The original and translation are "refracted through blue green black moss," an image combining a sense of earth, tree, water, and sky that has a distinct beauty but also can be a sign for how interpreters' perceptions of the two are *obscured*, perhaps necessarily. Also, in traveling "together to the margins of a cloud," the original and translation seem to be traveling toward a scene of indecipherability. After all, where does the sky's unclouded air really end and the "material" of a cloud begin? And even if such "margins" might be approximately discerned, do they "stand still" long enough to be "recorded"?

Although I, too, am in the position of translator or mistranslator, I would assert that the tropes of "cloud" and "margin" indicate an acknowledgment of what seems inevitably "lost" in the attempted translation of a so-called "original." In addition to the chance that an original manuscript will be materially lost, there is always the possibility that the original intention will be "lost" in the sense that the translator either does not know the differences between the "original language" and the "secondary language" as well as s/he thinks s/he does or that s/he consciously or unconsciously desires to translate the original in order to facilitate a certain reading, thus failing to allow the "original" interpretation of the text by the author and his/her designated community of readers to be transmitted to other readers and substituting what is substantially the translator's text. But how can we even speak of recuperating all the components of an "original" intention, since the author's consciously remembered intention may be less "real" than an inaccessible, unconscious one? In this sense, after the text is completed, the author is just another translator. Translation is inextricable from interpretation. The translator cannot get past interpretive conjecture to grasp definitively the origin and originality of the "original" text, the supposedly unified intention.

A "cloud" that obscures margins of understanding is in the way, and the translator or interpreter is in a position of belatedness or, as Shapiro puts it in the title of his 1977 book, *Lateness*. This belatedness, of course, can be conceived as an absence from supposed first principles in general and not only from the supposed first principle of a text. Interestingly, in canto IV of "Notes toward a Supreme Fiction," Wallace Stevens had used the trope of "clouds" in articulating the belatedness of poets and, implicitly, all other interpreters in relation to origins:

> The clouds preceded us
>
> There was a muddy centre before we breathed.

> There was a myth before the myth began,
> Venerable and articulate and complete.
>
> From this the poem springs: that we live in a place
> That is not our own and, much more, not ourselves
> And hard it is in spite of blazoned days.
>
> We are the mimics. Clouds are pedagogues.[13]

On the one hand, Stevens's speaker postulates the "dencetered," "marginally" uncertain trope of "clouds" as the origin of human interpretive striving, as well as an ur-myth, a "supreme fiction" and not a supreme truth. But on the other hand, he asserts—seemingly without irony—the priority an original *"center"* that, while "muddy," was "complete" or unified. Critics like Bové may read this apparent contradiction in terms as an indication that Stevens is exposing the impossibility of making a truth-claim for the prior existence of the "center"; nevertheless, the formulations may also point to the nostalgia for lost origins, indicating a belief in their absent unity. However, in allowing the priority and unity of the "original" to be undone again and again through the language of reversals and displacements and by avoiding "centralizing" declarations in "After a Lost Original," Shapiro forcefully indicates that a belated interpreter should not presume that there is an original unity beyond or before his/her perception, but rather that the unified concept of "origin" is too problematic to be accepted.

I had best not conclude a discussion of "After a Lost Original" without turning back to the possible reading of "original" and "translation" as "parent" and "child." At the time of writing, perhaps the two of them "live only together" in a physical dwelling, but, "refracted through [the] blue green black moss" of differing perspectives, "they travel together to the margins of a cloud"—that is, a "cloud" articulating the problems one faces in the interpretation of power relations in parent/child interaction, including the authority to represent the self and the other, the issue of psychological as opposed to chronological priority, and the determination of the margins between the two of them and those margins constituting both their bond as parent and child and their difference from the rest of the world. The once "venerable myth" of absolute patriarchal (or matriarchal) authority is now vulnerable to severe questioning, and thus the so-called "original" is forced to be "doubtful" about the received meanings of his/her "originating" position and even to consider the conceptual possibility of parental "belatedness" in relation to an offspring's desire for autonomy.

Shapiro's poetry is not only compelling when it challenges various concepts of origin and originality but when it assails various presumptions of totalized understanding. "The Lost Golf Ball" commences with a rather startling statement of loss:

> Part of the universe is missing
> Sings or says the newspaper, and I believe it.
> Even most of it. As tape runs out of a typewriter.
>   Big surprise:
> And it won't do to go looking for holes
> Or changes in the constitution of matter
> Like a rare jewel in a crossword puzzle
> Or yourself as an answer
> Linking and locking up space
> In the accidental field where you stumble
> Like a star lost on a white ceiling.
>
> (*HBA*, 35)

The poet generally resists the specious certitudes of journalistic discourse, but in this case, his speaker can "believe it" because the newspaper uncharacteristically gives news about uncertainty. The news, of course, is awkwardly put. If the uni-verse (literally, one turning) is the overall unity outside of which no life can exist, as opposed to a heterogeneous "multiverse," how can "part" of it be "missing"? The concept of the universe itself seems exposed as an inadequate explanatory term, since the perceptual apparatus of scientific experimentation—in the post-Heisenbergian era characterized by talk of "black holes"—cannot account for the complexities of space/time.

After admitting that "even most of" the universe might be "missing" rather than just a part, Shapiro's speaker whimsically compares the perceptual incompleteness to "tape" that "runs out of a typewriter." Perhaps sarcastically saying "big surprise," he notes that various attempts to retrieve what is missing will not succeed. One would "look for [black] holes" in vain, since they cannot be seen or experienced according to our ordinary notions of time and space. The individual "stumbling" in the continual experience of random connections and disconnections ("an accidental field") could hardly serve "as an answer," a solid plug for the great hole. The degree of abstract calculation needed even to estimate what is "missing" may exceed human capacity. Such superhuman complexity frustrates the hubristic desire for totalized understanding.

Repeating the poem's opening line in the plural, the speaker moves from a consideration of the supposed macrocosm to the microcosm of an individual human mind and then of a poem:

> Parts of the universe are missing
> The random minor stars you improvised
> Litter the mind but might not go out
> Damned to hell not what are you but
> Where are you my poem
> Nothing is left but the recantation.
>
> (HBA, 35)

The second line might comprise a trope for the "material" of the unconscious, which "might not" allow particular images and inexplicable thoughts (whether intriguing or merely "litter") to "go out" *coherently* into consciousness. On the other hand, "go out" might have the opposite sense of expiration. The lines could serve as a description of a kind of writer's block. Knowing that the material for a poem must exist in the unconscious and much too fragmentarily in consciousness, the poet finds the organizing force "missing" and asks it where it is. Amid the "hell" of thwarted expression, or a nomadic flow from word to word or phrase to phrase without criteria of inclusion and exclusion, only "the recantation" of the poetic impulse, an aura of absence painfully present, remains. The speaker then presents a perturbing string of phrases in apposition to the "recantation":

> The repetition in a glut
> Miraculous as evil
> Joining the democracy of pain to improve it
> A woman like Venice and like Venetian blinds

> Opening and closing
> Part of the universe is missing. Missing!
>
> (*HBA*, 35)

An excess of recurrent words or images in the mind refuses to be arranged. This "miracle" of disunity is compared (without explanation) to "evil" in its disruptive capacities, "joining the democracy of pain," which cannot be subsumed into a larger, benevolent order ("as if to improve it"). I must stress that "as" (comparison) is not "is" (identity): randomness is not considered equivalent to "evil," which is itself a "centered" concept. Randomness *precedes* and in fact can disorganize the binary opposition, good/evil. Harking back to the more sensitive use of Venetian blinds at the end of "To an Idea," the simile of the woman seems a parody of sexist reification of female sexual activity or childbirth. This seems to serve as an example of a simplistic, falsely metaphorical explanation of the universe's oscillations.

After a one-line strophe's further disruption, the longish final strophe of the poem meditates on its own title and the relation of titles to issues of representation:

> Is this our bedroom or a planetarium?
> The title could be an inducement like a lost ball
> though it never appears in the final painting
> though anything might, a buried ship, the title is a nude
> but the title is not a can opener or a handle for a pot
> Sometimes what is lost does make an appearance however
> taking a common revenge like a word
> Losing the lost golf ball, find the lost golf ball
> The title itself is a ceiling for
> stars that shine at night, will not fade, and stick by themselves
> like a slogan
> "You have made my room a universe," as you said you would.
>
> (*HBA*, 35–36)

The single-lined question suddenly wrenches the poem away from relatively abstract thinking about the universe and the mind and pinpoints a particular scene, though an ambiguous one. Anticipating the last line of the poem—since the intervening lines return to an abstract nonenvironment—we can imagine the universe represented pictorially on a bedroom ceiling or in a planetarium. But we are ahead of ourselves.

The tension between an enigmatic title and a work of art can be compared to the confusion caused by "part of the universe" being "missing." Whereas some might consider "the title . . . a can opener," an instrument to "open" the text to reveal a definitive reading "inside," "or a handle for a pot," something solid to "hold onto" in transporting the work from obscurity to a clearly demarcated context, the speaker of "The Lost Golf Ball" emphasizes how a title can create *difficulties* in interpretation, difficulties that may "induce" one to seek a solution. The inducement to find the "lost" relationship between title and work helps one "read" the work more carefully, as "a nude" in an art work may capture one's attention, only to lead the viewer to an expanded focus. Even the sudden "appearance" of the title in the work may not serve to articulate its relation to the painting or poem, if the former fails to harmonize in any way with other elements. One is directed by the speaker to "find the lost golf ball" and yet, paradoxically, the ball might still be "lost," a word rolling away from any single context, not discovered in any "hole" on the "green."

Nevertheless, we learn that "the title itself is a ceiling." Because of the dictates of literary convention, the title is literally an upper spatial limit for the poem, under which the words of the text, earlier compared to "stars," are allowed to "shine" without "fading" and can "stick by themselves" on the page during the "night" of a reader's scrutiny. Of course, one also thinks of the literal meaning of "stars," and so the use of "ceiling" and "stars" in the same context indicates that the reader is on the ground of fiction. Just as *representations* of stars are placed on a ceiling through a human being's arbitrary decision, a particular title sits above a poem's words because of an arbitrary decision on the part of the poet and not because some deity or "nature" itself has ordained it.

Distanced from authority by quotation marks—the only ones in the poem—the slogan expressing a ludicrous confidence in the ability of representation to fulfill its "promise" by reducing the vast universe to a two-dimensional pattern on the ceiling of someone's room is playfully parodied. I am reminded of the whimsical use of "heavenly bodies" in some of Joseph Cornell's boxes and of the little joke that ends Ashbery's long poem of many disjunctive and, at times, seemingly coherent collages, "The Skaters": "The constellations are rising / In perfect order: Taurus, Leo, Gemini."[14] If he thought about it, the individual gazing up at his own "starry" ceiling might surmise that "even most of . . . the universe is missing" from such a representation of it, if one can still employ the word "universe" unironically.

Can Shapiro's critiques—exemplified in such poems as "To an Idea," "After a Lost Original," and "The Lost Golf Ball"—of the pursuit of origins, originality, and totalization in attempts at representation be perceived as a general attack on all attempts at representation, as some have characterized the "postmodern" impulse? I do not think so. First of all, while the extremely disjunctive collage-poems described in my first chapter seem to reject many recognizable forms of representation by trying to avoid them, these poems of the 1980s can be shown to include somewhat coherent *representations* of notions of representation. The acceptance of such quasi-discursivity as an enabling condition in the poetry indicates either that discursivity itself and the possibility of relative degrees of provisionally accepted coherence, as opposed to particular absolutistic versions of representation, are not under attack or that one cannot dispense with such concepts and permit one's writing to be *legible*. In the poems I have discussed in this chapter, the naive sense that one can step outside representation into "pure" poetic "presentation"—creation *ex nihilo*—does not arise nor is there an implication that since attempts at representation have been responsible for immense distortions and coercions, *from now on* they should not be pursued in any form. The poetry, admittedly belated, neither advertises itself as an antipoetry or, arrogantly, as a *final* poetry (signifying the death of the genre or of literature itself) but as a kind of testing-ground, a site of investigation.

3
"Mirrors Rushing into Each Other"
The Poetics of Eros

In the erotic poetry of his mature years, David Shapiro has carefully and lucidly explored the representation of courtship, fierce passion, amatory power relations, and the uncertainties and ambivalences of heteroerotic entanglements. While the poems cannot be characterized as a feminist critique of patriarchal social constructions, they do include sharp parodies of masculinist or, to use Mary Ellman's term, "phallocratic," posturing.

Shapiro's preoccupation with erotic themes surfaces at the very beginning of his career. His early love poems, collected in *January*, are rather unified evocations of desire, freshened by occasional anomalous surreal fragments. In the book's title-poem, probably written when the poet was fifteen, the direct expression of erotic need strains against a stultifying atmosphere:

> I want you
> This morning is
> winter rocking
> my ear: there is no
> promise for it,
> but simultaneous
> and soft voices
> deprive, deprive.

(J, 20)

The tone, free-verse rhythm, and language are somewhat reminiscent of the "imagist" phase of William Carlos Williams, though the poem is less anchored in precise, sensory detail:

> No stain
> is on the streetlight

> between falling things
> and the hands only
> wave dusty loaves
> as the heart in
> her cone of cold
> waves the winter witch
> on all the boys
> making them wake and twitch.
>
> (20)

Next, Shapiro throws in the only enigmatic lines of the poem: "I want you, your hair and the puzzling / things your body / removes." What "puzzling / things" might he desire? The fragment is not developed, nor is it juxtaposed against other mysteries. The poem closes with a clearly articulated contrast between the restrictions of school and the pressure exerted by youthful desire:

> Is it winter
> The school is
> Thirty girls are running
> laughing to watch
> the teacher strain
> I cannot listen anymore
> because I want you
> because there is no name
> that morning recreates
> except yours
> because my feeling
> surrounds me
> I want you.
>
> (20)

In later poems, most notably "An Exercise in Futility," which I will discuss next, possible connections between erotic and pedagogical experience are drawn, but here the cognitive dimension of eros is deposed, even as the talk of what "morning" "names" has a slightly bookish tone. Never again does Shapiro risk the untempered sentimentality of the last six lines, but he continues in later work to concern himself with how the "feeling" of desire "surrounds" people.

"An Exercise in Futility," written nearly two decades after "January," begins by representing the quest for intellectual wisdom (occasioned by the contemplation of an ivory carving with a Taoist scene, as Shapiro has mentioned to me), displaces this quest with a highly metaphorical account of a sudden erotic pursuit of a woman, and just as suddenly shuttles back to a consideration of the carving and different ways of reading it. Through this juxtaposition, the erotics of learning and the study of erotics comment on each other's pursuit of desire.

Substituting "university professor" for "traveller" as the object of the main clause, "An Exercise in Futility" commences with a witty echo of the opening of Shelley's famous poem, "Ozymandias":

> I met an university professor in an antique land
> Who said: In my hand is a cartographer's dream,
> The country which blurred genres.
>   To release its secret of release
>
> Under the cartons of cardboard script, the discoverers, the learners,
> And one's own fingers exploring the dumb thick maps.
>   (*TI*, 17)

Rather than the fragmentary stone remnants of the statue of Ozymandias, "king of kings," in Shelley's poem, Shapiro turns the Taoist sage on the carving into "an university professor" discoursing on the map in his hands. This "cartographer's dream" is itself a "country," a new territory, a figure for a text, "which blurred genres," thus allowing the cartographer to accomplish more than the slavish representation of existing territory. One may recall Ashbery's *Three Poems* (1972), a long work in "prose" that includes much prosier elements than most earlier prosepoems, and to which Shapiro devoted an entire chapter in *John Ashbery: An Introduction to the Poetry.* Jasper Johns's paintings and drawings of maps, which both preserve and disturb the referential status of maps and of paintings with arbitrary placements and displacements of territory-names and of colors and with "loud" expressionist brushwork and obvious stencilling, are also relevant here. As Elizabeth Bishop, one of the twentieth-century American poets Shapiro appreciates most, quips in her early poem, "The

Map": "Are they assigned, or can the countries pick their colors?"[1]

With its repetition of "release" as a noun after a verb, the fourth line hints at connections between intellectual/aesthetic knowledge and carnal knowledge. Unveiling promises a release from ignorance, and so "discoverers" and "learners" search for the "secret" by groping for clues amid the "dumb thick" signs of the map. Suddenly, Shapiro's speaker apostrophizes eros:

> Oh secret love, heterodoxy, self-deceit,
> You have reckoned without the host and taken the shadow for
>   credulity
> And dreamt all the rapports, at the foot of the airmail letter.
> The nicety of a hair, the pleasures of exit
> Writhing in passages,
> Alive to the needle, down clever arches, hunting you like a bluejay.
>   (*TI*, 17)

Like the blurring of genres mentioned above, "secret love" (and "the secret of release" in love) may be a kind of "heterodoxy," an undermining of authoritarian order. There are specks of narrative: We do not learn how the "you" is caught in "self-deceit." Who is "the host" whom "you have reckoned without and whose "credulity" stands in relation to which "shadow"? Does the mention of "the host" add a religious tinge to the quest for erotic fulfilment? As in the collage-poems discussed in chapter 1, these lines resemble a map, like Johns's, whose place-names or boundaries between territories have been smudged. Possibly, though, the disjunction between the "you" and "the host" represents a disparity in intention between different parts of the same individual regarding the pursuit of love, and "the shadow" is not "credulity," but a potent unconscious impulse. The surreal notion of dreaming "all the rapports at the foot of the airmail letter" suggests the quixotic nature of the wish that one can "decode" full intimacy from a piece of writing—as one travels by consulting a map—and thus attain intimacy through this reading.

Oddly noting a trace of the beloved's presence, "the niceties of a hair," the speaker alludes to the quest for the fulfilment of desire in spatial terms: "exit," "passages," "arches." Note the spatial/literary pun on "passages," suggesting that the pursuit of love is like the erotic transport of a powerful reading experience. Along with the gerund "writhing," the phrase, "alive to the needle," as a straightforward kinesthetic trope and as a severe phallic image, evokes the sharp and perhaps dangerous intensity of the man's desire. If the simile, "hunting you like a bluejay," refers to the woman, it both flatters and reifies her, indicating that the speaker is pursuing "a rare bird," but the ambiguous syntax makes it equally possible that the man is comparing himself to the bluejay as comic "hunter."

At the beginning of the next strophe, the same kind of ambiguity is presented, then seemingly cleared up by the contextual information provided in the following clause, and yet complicated by several intricate tropes:

> You whom I had loved for years like a monumental door leading to
> An exterior interior: to get to this door you climbed a tiny, tinny podium
> And there two mirrors poured into each other
> In a maroon room covered up with dust of bricks and books:
> But for you the mirrors rushing into each other had lost something.
> (*TI*, 17)

Perceiving that the woman comes to the "monumental door leading to / An exterior interior," we may assume that the speaker's love for her is represented by the simile of the door. While, in the long history of patriarchal discourse, woman is almost always assigned the status of passive object and man that of active subject, in Shapiro's figurations, the woman actively enters the site of the man's desire, the "door" which leads to an "interior exterior," an area closer than any other to the possibility of a shared interiority (one might think of it as "interpenetration" rather than the masculinist-oriented "penetration") with the beloved and yet still outside—still at a threshold.

A "podium" is supposed to be a place of authoritative speech, where one-way communication can take place, but the speaker refers to this site as "tiny" and "tinny." By using these two adjectives to modify the noun "podium," Shapiro humorously points to the arbitrariness of language as a representational system, as he does with "maroon room," two lines later. The exposure of such arbitrariness can be said to unsettle authority: the podium does not collapse, but it hardly "towers." In fact, it is not the site of any sort of domination of an object by a subject—of a passive entity by an active one—but of "two mirrors" that "poured into each other." Does the trope imply an egalitarian interaction of active entities? Indeed, it deposes patriarchal representations of desire (and the reception of desire), but it also has a sinister side. If mirrors mirror each other in a sexualized "pouring" or "rushing," then the representations on their surface only represent other representations and not a "self" or worldly "reality." Indeed, as the woman apparently stated, "the mirrors . . . had lost something"—their usual purpose. This is "an exercise in futility": copies "rush" to copy each other, and the parody of intercourse does not result in a harmonious satisfaction of mutual desire, but expenditure without psychic gain.

In the following strophe, Shapiro returns abruptly to the scene on the ivory carving with the Taoist sage/"university professor." Desire, though, is still the theme:

I saw he had no temperament to speak of—
A fan instead of a typewriter, a tree that was watery air
Buoying the bright horizon; there other countries rolled up beside
    him;
And on the other side of him, a picture of him
Where he begs, student-wise, another sage,
For another scheme, like a part of the bending tree
Of desire. The beaks surround him
Surround us and lunge out of us like a wish.

(17)

The notion that the sage lacks a "temperament" suggests that he believes his "teaching" can only be achieved through an ascetic impersonality. Describing the scene on the ivory carving, the speaker notices the sage's "fan" and the almost surreal background of "a tree that was watery air / Buoying the bright horizon," transforming the usual sense of solidity to something much less stable. The desired "country which blurred genres" is not revealed; we are told that other maps (or "countries," as they are called) are "rolled up beside him."

Just as the poem's speaker had looked to the professor/sage as a learned guide, a vital part of the actualization of the "cartographer's dream," the professor himself is "captured" by a picture within the "picture" of the carving's scene—if you will, a map within the map—as the "begging" disciple of "another sage" who seems to be privy to "another scheme." This realization that individual (and, most likely, institutional) authority is merely a link in a chain without a discernible, unassailable origin casts doubt on the entire quest "to release [the] secret of" intellectual "release." This desire for release is perceived as an element in a continuum: "part of the bending tree of desire," like the strange tree in the scene. In all probability, the structure imposed on the erotics of learning, conveyed partly by this phallic trope, is criticized insofar as it is constituted by the structure of a patriarchal tradition and not by a community of *equally active* learners. Unlike the poem's two lovers, who each seemed to "beg" for each other's love and whose "mirrors poured into each other" without one of them attaining dominance, an authoritarian hierarchy of (seemingly male) learners places an individual in a subservient (passive) position before a sage, who must in turn humble himself before a "greater" sage. In actuality, of course, the wish for wisdom and for erotic fulfilment can never really be passive; even in the act of prostrating himself before a "sage," the "learner" is merely "containing" the active quality of a violent desire, a force existing both inside and outside, as evidenced by the vivid trope of "surrounding" and "lunging" "beaks," which teaches that desire cannot be hypostasized—one would like to "map" it, but it resists such attempts. The question that arises is whether the authority of coercive patriarchal structures can be sufficiently weakened by the subversions of desire.

In the final strophe of the poem, a calm tone pervades the description of other aspects of the carving:

> Snowflakes bewildered the upper edge of things.
> The bridge is not an argument.
> Nor is it a bridge, in a sense.
> The birds are flying buttresses.
> No impedimenta on the bridge;
> No traveller on the boardwalk; two hands are folded above the tree.
> (*TI*, 18)

The ambiguously rendered "bridge" represented on the carving, harking back to the "rapports" "dreamt of" earlier in the poem, does not establish an "argument" or bridge intellectual or erotic gaps. Literally, the representation of the "birds" (which surround the sage) on each side of the carving's chief scene "are flying buttresses." Taken as a trope and not merely as a description of a work of art, this image involves the "freezing" of figures of volatile desire into the figure of a solid basis for seemingly invariable stability. Since desire has been portrayed throughout the poem as an unsettling force that continually undergoes displacement, this is highly ironic. A bridge that is not a bridge, "in a sense" (as a literal, *sensory* entity), is supported by "buttresses" that are not only "flying" in the conventional architectural sense but figuratively mimic the flying of the birds represented. The abundance of linguistic play cannot be relied upon to "buttress" anything solid and unchanging.

Once again a "literal" description of imagery on the carving, the "two hands . . . folded above the tree" can be interpreted either to surmount the tree as patriarchal representation of desire with a higher (Taoist?) authority, or to protect it serenely from inclement weather. The "two hands" are detached from the rest of a human body, like the cast body parts in some of Jasper Johns's collage-works. This detachment undermines the hands' possible status as a trope of reassurance or authority. In keeping with its title, the poem represents "an exercise in futility," in the sense that "the secret of release" has continually eluded erotic and intellectual seekers. Not only does this poem join such texts as "The Lost Golf Ball" in its critique of the quest for the "secret," representable totalization, but it indicates that the quest for "carnal *knowledge*" as a statically and ahistorically definable entity is mystified.

Shapiro's most sustained contemplation of the erotic occurs in the six-page poem, "A Song." Using the title of the 1960s soul classic "When a Man Loves a Woman" by Percy Sledge as a frequent refrain, the poem explores the use of hyperbolic rhetoric in the representation of passion. Performed in a hauntingly soulful style, Sledge's song catalogs various ways in which a lovelorn man will go to extreme lengths to woo, win, and hold a woman and will suffer nearly unimaginable abuse. If Sledge intends any irony, it is not apparent in his rendering. Shapiro's much longer text pays parodic homage to and presents a parodic deflation of the song's intensity and language; it baroquely exaggerates its "precursor's" exaggerations and tilts them in strange new directions. "A Song" begins with a surreal impression of the power of words of love:

> When a man loves a woman
> the words withdraw to the palace
> he demands his words and rejoices seeing them neighing
> > into his face
> the words in whiteness the words race the hasty words
> > stand around and excite their breasts
>
> When a man loves a woman
> He wraps his coat of words about his shoulders
> Scaled with gold and white mountain words
> At the same time he fits for wearing both his word and his world
>
> When a man loves a woman
> he seizes the strong word with violence and says trembling
> Now Oh word never disappearing
> Now the world is present and the maximum Actor wrote you (not
> > spoken)
>
> When a man loves a woman
> the words preside over the pool and the surrounding streams
> the king of the sky spits and the nymph grace note
> of rivers grace note to my mind you know I have
> > > preferred you alone to all placed you
> > > willingly in a part of
> > > my words
>
> WHEN A MAN LOVES A WOMAN BY PERCY SLEDGE
>
> > > > > > > > > > (TI, 31)

In the opening quatrain, the lover's desire for the presence of his own erotic rhetoric seems to parallel his desire for the woman. He is in love with the manifestations of his own expressiveness and "rejoices" in their comically horselike reappearance from "the palace" (the woman or wider circulation?). In their speed—echoed by the breathless, onrushing quality of the poem's unpunctuated lines—and their ability to "stand around," "the words in whiteness" of a page seem to have a sexual impact on the *general* environment: "excite *their* breasts"—not only the one beloved's. The lover's words are also a kind of clothing, a source of protection for him from (external) emotional coldness, as well as an item for ostentatious display: "Scaled with gold and white mountain words." Not only does the man want to "wear" his "word" but also his "world," in the sense that the all-encompassing tropes and tone of his amorous expression makes him think that the entire world can be reduced (through synecdoche) to his own scale.

In the third quatrain, the "violent" "seizing" emphasizes the man's will to power even more directly. When the speaker apostrophizes the "word," he tries to assert the supreme fictions of its permanent impact and of the full "presence" of the "world" in it. If the "maximum Actor" is meant to stand for a supreme being, it might signify one who takes the most wide-ranging worldly actions, but it may just as easily evoke one who maximally stages dramatic *fictions*. Like an actor, the lover described here operates on the basis of a determined role, but the speaker emphasizes that the "Actor" "wrote" the world—"(not spoken)." This may allude to Derrida's deconstructive reversal (in *Of Grammatology* and elsewhere) of the traditional privileging of speech in the binary opposition, speech/writing, suggesting that the "world" and "love" are always constructed as a scene of textuality, a structure of mediation that does not accomplish the recuperation of full presence. Hence, in the quatrain that follows, "the words preside over" various bodies of water, and the music that emanates from them, as well as the ornamental "grace note," while rain is represented unromantically by the vulgar image of "the king of the sky [spitting]." Words preside over the "negotiation" of love.

Stepping into the lover's role for the first time, the speaker does not praise the woman, but following the lead of certain Renaissance love-sonneteers (if more awkwardly), he suggests to her how lucky she is to be singled out to be "placed . . . willingly in a part of [his] words." Throughout this opening part of the poem, a flamboyant egotism—exemplifying the masculinist notion of the expression of love as a "seamless" rhetorical performance delivered to the passive (silent) female—is flagrantly exposed, along with the seams of rhetoric.

In the next several quatrains, the exploration of hyperbole takes a quirky new trajectory:

When a man loves a woman
Hospitals are supplied with beds and clothing
If she is life nearer the front
He is fitted with beds kitchens and dispensaries

When a man
the sick and wounded upon their hands like wagons

He gives his ambulance
he is incapable of keeping up with the troops. . . .

When a man loves a woman
the wounded man is transferred to a hospital ship
in the comfortable swinging cot in the airy ward
and the ice flies into the hot wind and the bed rises on the shore.
(*TI*, 31–32)

"When a man loves a woman," he imagines the force of that love to be so immense that unrelated practical problems are solved—magically and immediately. The patriarchal notion of woman as all-bountiful nurturer (amid the destructive ambience of male war on land and sea) is entertained and parodied.

Even the male lover, self-centered as the speaker has portrayed him, is supposedly made compassionate by his passion for the beloved: seeing a war's "sick and wounded upon their hands like wagons"—a joltingly comic image—"He gives his ambulance" and, consequently, lags behind "the troops," perhaps in ferocity as well as in their covering of ground. Amid these unsettling references to war scenes, the surreal images of transformation involving "ice" and "the bed" temper the debunking impact of parody with a tone of nobility in representing the rise of erotic impulses. While the poet desires to depose the overblown rhetoric of passion, he still wants, in part, to celebrate the fecundity and beauty of passion itself: "When a man loves a woman a genus of the trees / Parts of the world are fruit / Used for good and light" (33).

Parodying the element of complaint about the woman's unattainability in many Renaissance love poems, numerous sections of "A Song" suggest that the lover requires desperate, body- and soul-breaking efforts to win the beloved. Feeling the need "to outstrip the wind on an automobile," the man, figured as a high-ranking military officer with Cupid's equipment, finds that "equipment" exceedingly inadequate for amatory conquest:

> When a man loves a woman
> he beholds her far off like a headquarters
> first having pursued her through the void
> through the long void with a short arrow.
>
> (33)

In the contemporary context of automotive culture, the actions of the male take on more of a ridiculous than a "heroic" cast:

> When a man loves a woman
> he stops his Toyota and leaps from his front seat
> and comes up to her half dead with a safety belt
> and his neck being pressed with her foot he wrenches
> > the wrench from her right hand
>
> And dips it shining in his alto jugulo (throat).
>
> (TI, 34)

These lines make light of the patriarchal notion that man is capable of "protecting" and should try to protect woman. The context is laughably unclear. Which of the two is "half dead"? Is the woman in a car, underneath the car, fixing it with a "wrench," or elsewhere, and what good can the "safety belt" do for her when she may not be in a moving vehicle? What purpose does it serve—for either of them—when "he wrenches the wrench from her right hand"? Is the wrench a trope of phallic power? And if so, what hetero-, homo-, or auto-erotic impact does this have when the man "dips it shining in his . . . (throat)"? The multiple confusions of the passage help strip the male of any authority as rescuer of a "damsel" who is not necessarily in "distress" but might be doing very well without him.

In contrast to the sections in which military tropes are privileged ("When a man loves a woman / he attacks the fleet"), at various points in "A Song" there is a sense that certain tropes are beginning to articulate the man's physical vulnerability to the effects of passion. As elsewhere in Shapiro's work, the male lover's submission to pleasure/pain is sometimes textualized:

> When a man loves a woman
> his neck is untouched and suddenly the words are
>   humming in his carcass like bees
> and his dissolved entrails breaking through the page
> and immense clouds of words are drawn out.
>
> (35)

Metaphorically, the male "body" becomes a "carcass" in the sense that its solidity is made to "dissolve" and be transformed into a site of heterogeneous, vibrating activity. As in Helene Cixous's and in Gilles Deleuze's and Felix Guattari's depositions of Jacques Lacan's notion of desire as lack, Shapiro's speaker figures desire as an assembling of forces. (And, of course, it can be said that the poem's instances of parodic critique have been leveled at deadening or stultifying reifications of this process.) In "Dead Psychoanalysis: Analyze," Gilles Deleuze and Claire Parnet provide an apt gloss for the various representations of the dynamic assemblages of desire in "A Song":

Desire only exists when assembled or machined. You cannot grasp or conceive of a desire outside a determinate assemblage, on a plane which is not pre-existent but must itself be constructed. . . . Desire . . . is made up of different lines which cross, articulate or impede each other and which constitute a particular assemblage on a plane of immanence.[2]

In the concluding quatrains of "A Song," the assemblages of eros are linked to a call for the nurturance of ecological assemblages:

> When a man loves a woman
> grapes increase hair and spontaneous flourishes elsewhere
> but the stones are established in the empty globe
> whence a woman a hardy race was produced
>
> When a man loves a woman
> the prospect may feed the hungry mind but the land will not give
> also you will ask what depth the trenches
> Do not commit the vine even to the light furrow the earth is low

> When a man loves a woman
> it sinks its roots into the Hall
> and for many years strong arms and branches move this way and that
> Nor let your yard incline nor plant the lazy hazel among the vines nor break the twigs (love the earth).
>
> (*TI*, 36)

With a surreal touch of humor, "grapes" are said to create an (indirect) erotic impact. If the "stones" can be read as eggs in a primal womb responsible for the "production" of "woman a hardy race," they could just as easily signify another, less determinate source of primordial solidity. As in "After a Lost Original," we are distanced from the authority of origins. The mention of "grapes," "stones," and "globe" leads to a speedy, only partly discursive consideration of our endangered environment, "the land" which cannot be controlled by the amorous "hungry mind" and which "will not give." Is the speaker suggesting that "the land will not give" food or that it refuses to give according to human desires that do not take its own natural laws into account? The poet warns of the grave danger which our ecosystem faces: "Do not commit the vine even to the light furrow the earth is low."

While, at the poem's beginning, the male lover's "words withdraw to the palace," at its close, his love "sinks its roots into the Hall"—perhaps the palace's hall. In this juxtaposition of tropes, "nature" infiltrates "unnatural" architecture, or perhaps the "hall" can be construed as the psychological space separating the two individuals. "For many years," the motions of "strong arms and branches" perpetuate erotic passion. Coming directly after these lines of erotic rooting and movement, the speaker's final admonition (to the reader, lover, and beloved) to take care of the natural environment and to "love the earth" links eros and ecology as fundamental "assemblages" that foster the perpetuation of life.

Those who lump Shapiro's poetry and poetics with Ashbery's ignore that the older poet comes much closer to the devaluation of all values that characterizes various strains of nihilism, as in the treatment of political commitment and lack of it in "The Skaters."[3] Shapiro—despite the prominent negativity of his critiques of forms of representation and in keeping with his political affiliations discussed in my introductory chapter—frequently and vigorously affirms such values as social equality, individual freedom, collaborative work, and respect for natural processes in his writing. If Ashbery ever included a phrase like "Love the earth" in a poem, it would be deflated by irony, whereas Shapiro gives no indication at the end of "A Song" that an ironic attitude toward the phrase is appropriate. In "A Song," ironies have been reserved, not for "love" or "passion," but for particular representations of them and for the egocentric perspectives sometimes motivating those representations.

Shapiro's mature poetry includes a great deal of ambivalence about erotic experience: the dangers of "an expense of spirit" and possible betrayals are considered alongside positive assemblages of desire. This ambivalence is richly evident in "You Are Tall and Thin," written in 1989 and part of the sequence, "After a Lost Original," mentioned earlier. Shapiro calls the poem a deliberate mistranslation and collaging of elements from a cycle of Spanish folksongs from the Andalusian region. Apparently, these songs influenced the poetry of Lorca, Alberti, Jiminez, Machado, and other major Spanish poets. With its extremely varied line-lengths and its unpredictable strophic pattern, "You Are Tall and Thin" displays a complex musical effect that pays homage to the beauty of the Andalusian songs:

In the circle of the sky
I disembark quietly: You were wrong.
They call this the street
where a single dove made a difference, where we galloped over
    each other like
car tires.

The song says You are tall and thin
like your mother.
In the seance that follows, you sell
my dirty body.

Does it hurt to mix yourself up with conquistadors
So many hands, so many javelins, so many burials
like the photograph of an error.

Throughout the night, the song thinks

this is it
And often you live like a simulation
shopping for eyes.[4]

The surreal image opening the poem sets a romantic scene, which is immediately disturbed by the speaker's announcement that he has "disembarked" from this circular "vessel" and that "You [probably the beloved] were wrong." The context of her perceived error and its relation to his departure from the "circle" are not articulated, and this makes the speaker's simple declaration all the more ominous. In the next couplet, the speaker, having departed from a celestial realm, returns to a scene of the lovers' past encounter, a "street." The notion that "a single dove made a difference" on that street (with its traditional evocation of the dove as a trope of peace) contrasts strikingly with the rather violent eroticism of "where we galloped over each other like / car tires." This phrase is reminiscent of traces of sadomasochistic fantasy in such earlier poems as "The Cures of Love"—"You beat me to a powder. / You smeared my brow with crushed onions . . . / And tied a flour sack around my head" (*PT*, 23)—and less obviously in "The Night Sky"—"I would thread with a hook and eye your dress / Fasten you to me with a rod or a bolt / Pass through like a curtain rod your eyes / And they never shut" (*PT*, 8). The image of the "galloping . . . tires" is neither a sign of patriarchal man's subjugation of woman nor of a possible feminist egalitarianism, but of the mutual enactment of love/hate, creation/destruction. Whereas cars and car motors are often used as tropes for passion, the strange development of "car tires" (mixed as a simile with "galloped") tends to puncture an aura of romanticism with the "pressure" of the ordinary, as in the music of John Cage, the lightbulb and beer can sculptures of Jasper Johns, and the sculptural collages of Robert Rauschenberg. The extreme length of the line joining the "single dove" and the "car tires" seems to point to a prolongation of simultaneous pleasure and pain.

The next strophe shifts to a whimsically oedipal citation of one of the Andalusian songs—as though the archetypal picture of a mother is "tall and thin" any more than it is short and stout—and then darkly introduces the notion of the commodification (and hence betrayal) of erotic relations: "In the seance that follows, you sell / My dirty body." Although it is not clear who is "living" and who is "dead" in the "seance," it seems obvious that the relationship has suffered a severe "disconnection," and the man feels his body has been "dirtied" by the experience. In the next line, infidelity is established as the culprit. Probably exercising her own desire for power in breaking out of the implied contract of monogamy, the woman is subject to (mixed up with) *conquistadors'* desire for domination, and the speaker asks whether this involvement "hurts." In this context, multiplicity is figured as phallic impalement or, less likely, the woman's own thrusting ("so many javelins") and loss ("so many burials"). The simile, "like the photograph of an error," which puns on the Latin derivation of "error," "wandering," suggests that distancing or mediation accrues from the experience of this erotic multiplication and blunts intensity.

Echoing Ashbery's use of pronouns without determinate antecedents, the first two lines of the fifth strophe pictures the beloved, represented as "the song," fixating on a particular nocturnal encounter as the realization of the vague quintessence she had always been seeking ("thinks / this is it"). But the temporal specificity of "throughout the night" indicates that this illusion passes quickly. The speaker laments the woman's attitude in the terms of Jean Baudrillard's concept of "simulation" in "post-modern" society and recent artists who often utilize Baudrillard's work as a theoretical justification for their own probing of such topics as "commodity fetishism." According to Baudrillard,

The space of simulation confuses the real with the model. There is no longer any critical and speculative distance between the real and the rational. There is no longer really even any projection of models in the real . . . but an in-the-field, here-and-now transfiguration of the real into model. A fantastic short circuit: the real is hyperrealised.[5]

Shapiro's speaker in "You Are Tall and Thin" notes that the addressed beloved often "lives" as though she is not a human being but is conforming to a "hyperrealised" model of a human being, for whom perception (and other sensory and intellectual experiences) is not a matter of the individual effort of critical and creative reflection but the purchasing of a mass-produced commodity. Shapiro is not valorizing the sociological observations of Baudrillard and the "commodity fetishist" artists like Jeff

Koons, Ashley Bickerton, and Haim Steinbach in their suggestions about the inevitability of simulated experience in contemporary culture; *his speaker* implies that the woman being addressed "often" (not always) *limits herself* to this posture.

In the rest of the poem, the speaker further explores his ambivalence about his relationship with the beloved, whose beauty and power have both sinister and seductive aspects:

> I crossed the riddle,
> Caring about the colors, water purple and orange.
>
> Plunging like an elevator into an envelope
> All these letters, your branches, fragrant Rhada.
>
> While I wake slowly as a child
> You are tall and thin, on the bed where
> you play so well.
>
> You are high and delegate authority
> like a lake.
> The night dies like a ninny on the wall.
>
> At night you burn like the library of Alexandria.
> In the morning, you are Alexandria, in a mirror.
> You are so black you are white, like a firefly in sunlight.

Having crossed (and not necessary solved) "the riddle"/river/ rio of the woman's elusiveness, the speaker seeks the vibrant intensity of secondary "colors, water purple and orange." Chaotic passion deranges the common sense of spatial organization: "Plunging like an elevator into an envelope." Also, the obvious suggestion of sexual intercourse is disrupted by the fact that the "elevator," assigned the position of the phallus, consists of an interior that opens and closes, like the vagina and the "envelope." Even though the former is doing the "plunging" into the latter, the "masculine" figure *could be entered* just as easily: a woman might "enter" the psychological "interior" of a man. The arrangement of tropes can be said to call attention to the arbitrariness of the literal reading of sexual intercourse as man's domination of woman, an outside occupying an inside.

Because of the ambiguity created by a lack of punctuation between the lines of the couplet in question, "all these letters" may or may not be directly related to (for instance, a product of) the "plunging." In any case, there is a kind of "dissemination," a ramifying multiplication of communications that may, through its excess, thwart contact between the speaker and the woman. While, earlier in the poem, she is associated with Spain through the mention of *conquistadors,* now she is figured as the "fragrant" lover of the Hindu deity, Krishna, and, a few lines later, a simile and a metaphor place her in an Egyptian context. Taken together, these universalizing gestures undermine themselves; the specific woman eludes accurate representation.

Expressing both admiration for and dismay about the woman, and calling some attention to their own inadequacy in characterizing her, enigmatic similes and metpahors persist until the end of the poem. After calling the woman "tall and thin" once again, but now "on the bed where you play so well," the speaker mentions that she "delegate[s] authority," perhaps referring to how she delegates roles to men in sex-play. But in her ability to delegate, she is quirkily compared to "a lake," which forms the beginning of a second simile. The lake acts as a mirror "authorizing" reflections—for instance, "The night dies like a ninny on the wall." As the night "dies" when "replaced" on the surface of a lake by dawn, the male "ninny" "dies" (in the sexual sense) on/in the woman's (internal) "wall," according to the authority she grants him. The connections are legible enough not to appear meaningless, but tenuous and wild enough to indicate that the "essence" of the woman and her interaction with the speaker cannot be fully comprehended.

As for the woman's erotic bliss, her body is figured as a vast assemblage of wisdom at the point of decomposition: "At night you burn like the library of Alexandria." In the history of patriarchal literature, "Woman" is often made a figure of the embodiment of wisdom in order to indicate, in part, that actual women are incapable of appropriating wisdom through intellectual activity. Shapiro's speaker, on the other hand, immediately undermines this old left-handed idealization with the follow-up: "In the morning, you are Alexandria, in a mirror." After the experience of passion, the woman rises out of her "burning" to "become" a metaphor (mirror) for the entire city and not only the library or its ruins. "Inside" or "outside" these tropes, the actual woman may be playing hide and seek. Resisting static definition, she is assigned both of the absolute poles of the color spectrum in the final one-line strophe of the poem: "You are so black you are white, like a firefly in sunlight." If the firefly is not "invisible" in sunlight, it is almost impossible to separate as a figure from its blazing ground.

Sometimes in Shapiro's poetry, uncertainty brings with it a pleasurable, even ecstatic taste of freedom; here, for the poem's speaker, it brings an anxious ambivalence about erotic experience. In the course of the poem, the speaker seems to resume an earlier pursuit of his beloved and resignedly acknowledges their great distance from one another. Does the lover see the beloved as she "is," as a self-produced "simulation," or as a "simulation" he has constructed, or does he know her absence "in the seance that follows" their encounter? Does he know only his failure to know her? Does the speaker place himself in the authoritative position of the woman's "critic," or does he realize that his imperfect understanding of her undermines that authority? I believe that the poem raises these questions more than it answers them, largely because of disjunctions between (and sometimes within) the speaker's various "pronouncements" and expressions of uncertainty. In any case, I am not led as a reader either to accept or deny his "versions" of the woman's behavior or "self," but only to refuse the "superior" position of judgment. Complicity with the judgment of a human being is always problematic, but how is a "trial" even conceivable when the woman is not given a voice in the text?

In "An Exercise in Futility," "A Song," "You Are Tall and Thin," and other, similar poems, Shapiro does not naively attempt to offer a totalizing transcription of unspeakable erotic bliss, nor does he presume to "capture" the "mystery" of the "Other," nor does he reaffirm centuries of masculine privilege in erotic relations by striving to reerect the "Phallus" as "Transcendental Signifier" or "Signified." Not only renouncing these extremely dubious projects, which are rampant in the history of love poetry by males, but subjecting them to parodic critique and hinting at alternative ways of writing the erotic, he helps clear the ground for other poets (female and male) to concentrate on the representation of egalitarian heteroerotic relations.

4
"The Pluralism of Possible Styles"
A Reading of "The Devil's Trill Sonata"

In *Jim Dine: Painting What One Is,* David Shapiro states that for the painter, "it has not been a military choice between mimesis and antimimesis, between imitation and the self-reflective mode." Dine has created "an art that is always both imitative and self-referential and one that gains its sensual strength both by rigorous constraints and plural pleasures." Here Shapiro could be speaking about himself. As I have tried to demonstrate in the previous chapters, both "mimesis and antimimesis"—a mimesis that does not attempt to replicate questionable, prior forms of representation and an antimimesis that never arrogantly strives to annihilate all representation—are important to Shapiro's poetic project. Just as Dine can be said to bring together "a realism and a Surrealism that is not a reverie but what Walter Benjamin called for: *profane illumination,*" and just as "he has fought to escape escapism, but has always been charmed enough to know the necessity for a theory of escape,"[1] I would assert that strong elements of surrealism do not make Shapiro's poetry dominantly surrealist, hints of Dada do not make it Dadaist, partial celebrations of linguistic and erotic pleasure do not make it hedonist, and elements of mourning and social protest do not make it dominantly elegiac or politically moralistic. More severely than in Eliot's *The Waste Land,* where "fragments" are "shored against . . . ruins,"[2] and yet not as uncompromisingly as in Ashbery's "Europe" (and other poems in *The Tennis Court Oath*), the collaging of many different and often disparate materials in Shapiro's mature poetry *deletes* the narrative, emotive, and/or meditative continuities often taken for granted in lyric poetry. At the same time, the poems offer a wide array of tones, moods, tempos, linguistic surfaces, and "tastes" and disruptions of themes.

Shapiro is interested in the investigation of what he calls in his book on Dine "the pluralism of possible styles of rendering,"[3] the exploration of various aesthetic, cognitive, and other desires, and the constellation of various implicit and explicit themes in opposition and apposition. Such pluralist exploration can be seen as an affirmation of multiplicity. In their essay "Rhizome," Gilles Deleuze and Felix Guattari, collaborative critical theorists whom Shapiro has cited favorably in discussion and in writing, utilize the "rhizome" as a trope for a potentially limitless, centerless multiplicity, irreducible, they claim, either "to the One or the Many" and connecting

> any point with any other point. . . . It is not made of units but of . . . shifting directions. It has neither beginning nor end, but always a middle, through which it pushes or overflows. . . . [T]he rhizome is made only of lines: lines of segmentation and stratification as dimensions, but also lines of flight or deterritorialization as the maximal dimension according to which, by following it, the multiplicity changes its nature and metamorphoses. . . . [The] rhizome refers to a map that must be produced or constructed, is always detachable, connectable, reversable, and modifiable, with multiple entrances and exits, with its lines of flight.[4]

As in Deleuze and Guattari's description of the "rhizome," there is a similar sense of continual transformation in reading and rereading Shapiro's long poems—as though one is perpetually in the "middle." This "rhizomatic sensibility"—this multiplicity that never settles for a thematic or affective center but endlessly modifies the "direction" of its lines in processes of "segmentation," "stratification," "deterritorialization," and "reterritorialization"— is most impressively evident in the long poem, "The Devil's Trill Sonata" (Lateness), named after a piece by Tartini, an eighteenth-century violinist. Although, as I noted in my introduction, this three-sectioned poem begins with a six, then a seven-line strophe and proceeds with eighty-seven quatrains (and a single tercet in the middle), the stanzaic regularity is offset by a tremendous variety of musical effects. Subtle rhymes and off-rhymes appear and disappear. While the lines are predominantly long, they vary considerably in length and in the pattern of lengths in a given stanza, and there is an abundance of subtle and dramatic rhythmic and tonal shifts.

The first section of "The Devil's Trill Sonata" begins with a "perturbing" collage of a kind of invocation/quotation/invitation and its sharp deflation, a surreal narration that comments uncannily on the invocation, and an odd elegiac supplement:

> As Aeschylus puts it
> in Frag. 351: Let us say what comes to our lips,
>   whatever it
> may be; or perhaps, Let's say what's on
> the tip of our tongue.
>   As Achilles put it to Apollo,
> You have made a fool of me.
>
> It was with some interest
> I noticed the violin back in its case
> of itself, was playing the piece
> correctly and with almost
> no trepidation of the string!
> It played and is playing
> by and of and for itself—
>
> And that was the end of our friend
> The wisest and best on this earth lightly inclined—
> "Be mute for me,
> contemplative violin."

While the initial citation from Aeschylus seems to grant permission for this long poem to consist of free-associations, the second version of it is a jarring paradox: how can people "say what's on / the tip of [the] tongue" when the phrase itself signifies the inability to articulate a particular thought that is "below" the conscious level? Whenever one tries to achieve linguistic spontaneity or somehow arrive at the "language" of the unconscious, there is always the risk of seeming foolish, as the additional reference to the slow-witted warrior Achilles being outfoxed by the sun god Apollo suggests. In this opening stanza of "The Devil's Trill Sonata," perhaps the poet is signaling that he would like the work to appear as spontaneous as possible without seeming foolish. On the one hand, what follows includes highly disjunctive collages fostering wild leaps of association; on the other hand, the fact that there are many quatrains (and rhymes) obviously runs counter to the spontaneous impulse.

The little tale of the violin acting as virtuoso violinist "by and of and for itself" takes the notion of self-generated, "spontaneous" art-making to an absurd extreme and thus casts doubt on the idealization of automatic writing and of the unconscious "speaking for itself" (by some surrealists and their followers). When poets, speaking of "inspiration," exclaim that a poem has "written itself," this can be interpreted as the expression of a sense of a *relative* absence of conscious control over the writing process, but, when it is taken as an absolute, a supreme fiction, is it any less ridiculous than the self-playing violin? The "elegiac" statement in the first of the poem's many quatrains has a fruitful ambiguity: "our friend" who has met "the end" could be the superfluous human violinist watching the violin doing his/her job (in a self-lacerating nightmare), or it could be the violin standing for the dream of spontaneous creation. In either case, some unspecified speaker asks the "contemplative violin" to "be mute" for him.

No sooner has this fiction become "mute" than the poem moves on to a series of different physical motions. This is similar to the sprightly and often bizarre physics experiments in Shapiro's previous long poem, "About This Course." At first there is a confidence in the results of a speedy process—"You clamp the rifle and release the bullet / And you know that it will always reach the target"—but then the speaker acknowledges the impingement of unpredictable factors in processes: "What course must the aviator set / On a level road when the day is wet?" In the rhyme of these lines, "wet" can be said to undermine the "setness" of "set" and call upon the need for adjustment, or reset. What Deleuze and Guattari call "deterritorialization," the rupturing or displacement of one context on account of the often sudden (and in some way conflicting) entrance of another (or others), is thematized through humorous and striking images: "The tracks of the raindrops on the window / Are dropped from the bridge by a boy. // . . . A stone is seen to pass through the window / But now the stone is snow." The poet speeds up and attaches energetic surreal metaphors to natural processes in order to highlight the sudden impact of transformation: "The flower leaves the stem like an aviator / Or like the man in the elevator // The milkweed fills the sky."

Even in the collages of Eliot's *The Waste Land*, the suggestive use of the five section-titles and of recurrent phrases gives the reader the sense of gathering an overall meaning while moving, despite stops and starts, from a beginning, through a middle, to the end—with its final blessing. In "The Devil's Trill Sonata," the "rhizomatic" collaging of fragmentary descriptions and narrations does not result in the "blessing" of a perceived unity. Continually, the reader may find him/herself stuck in a "middle" or in an arbitrary pseudo-beginning, neither of which comes to closure but is interrupted by another middle or pseudo-beginning or a pseudo-closure that offers neither a final or a provisional resolution, but only further uncertainty. (Disjunction is not nearly as extreme as in poems like "The Heavenly Humor" or "Poems from Deal," described in my first chapter, nor does "The Devil's Trill Sonata" achieve disjunctive effects through the decomposition of syntax, as does Ashbery's "Europe" and other poems in *The Tennis Court Oath*.) Nevertheless, amid this uncertainty, there may be a salient connection between a couple of fragmentary narrations, not one that establishes a lasting, overarching unity, but a loose, *temporary* analogy that helps structure the development of a poetic "multiplicity" until a new "deterritorialization" occurs, so that, once again, "the multiplicity" transforms itself. Take, for instance, the different evocations of the disagreeable necessity of encountering some authority figure in the following four quatrains:

> What flower do most people go far to avoid?
> You are beginning to find a bed very boring
> Yet you are not allowed to sit up more than an hour at a time.
> Mother stands straight up at Green's Five and Ten Cent store.
>
> A supply of white floating soap, and you are all ready to carve up
> This tray holds all I need;
> It's a nice clean occupation.
> But I am not sure what these incalculable beasts may do.
>
> You need a ticket of admission to my rooms.
> Naomi and I make up contrite items and float them down the
>   stairs.

You are lying on your back in the honeysuckles—choking.
My entire life was being decided by five nincompoops.

Father says, I will get you a glass of water
If you will bring me a leaf from the linden.
So you ran to the linden tree, crying Dear linden, dear linden,
Give me one of your leaves.

After raising a strange question about avoidance (of a flower), the speaker addresses some patient who is required, probably by a medical authority, to lie in bed and observe "very boring" rules of recovery. Although this "you" is not identified, it may be the poet's mother, the subject of two elegies in *Lateness*, who, in the next line, is pictured standing "straight up" at a store. According to this interpretation, the poet/speaker expresses his empathy with his mother, perhaps in a memory of what he actually said to her or wished to say. He aligns himself with her in her desire to rebel against the doctor's unfeeling (and seemingly infantilizing) authority. (The later poem, "Friday Night Quartet," begins with the quatrain: "My mother said, / All surgeons want to do is surge. / And as one took the staples from her skull / She said, Neurosurgeons are not nice" [*TI*, 67].) Directly after this expression of solidarity, the poet recalls an earlier image of his mother standing "straight up," unconstrained by illness and doctors in the context of her domestic life, and shifts to a third-person narration, which distances the image from the woman's present state. The movement from "you" to "she" shows how Frieda Shapiro is turned from an active subject to an "object," a convalescent. No commentary tells us how heartbreaking the juxtaposition of two different images of the same person might be, but we may infer it.

In the next quatrain, an "I" speaks about his/her experience. It is hard to say whether it could be Mrs. Shapiro, the poet, or anyone else, but the sudden reference to soap seems to spring (associatively) from the prior reference to "Green's Five and Ten Cent store." The speaker seems to be defending the soap—perhaps an emblem of purity and cleanliness in an unsatisfactory environment—from a "you" who "are all ready to carve" it "up." In addition, "incalculable beasts" are thought to menace the speaker, who may be articulating a paranoid delusion or simply reacting with whimsical hyperbole ("This tray holds all I need") to incursions on his/her autonomy.

Without any resolution to this uncertainty, the reader is dumped into the middle of another situation in which a reaction to authority plays a part. Here, it seems that a precocious child contests parental control by speaking of "a ticket of admission." But in the quatrain's second line, the speaker and "Naomi," the actual name of one of Shapiro's three sisters, display their partial susceptibility to parental power when they engage in a strange, mediated ritual of "penance" ("contrite items") from the safety of their "fortress." Perhaps this act of apology includes an aspect of defiance, since the "floating" of the items—recalling "a supply of white floating soap" five lines earlier—might disrupt family tranquility (with a mess) more than it restores harmony. Without even a line's continuation of the skimpy narrative thread, another scenic disjunction occurs. Some unspecified "you" is suffocating—perhaps physically this time, and not emotionally—"in the honeysuckles." The following line jumps suddenly to the perspective of an "I" railing against "five nincompoops." The poem is dated "1973–1974," and during that time, Shapiro defended his doctoral dissertation at Columbia University, where, in humanities departments, five professors examine the student's work. On the other hand, there were five other members of the poet's household when he was growing up. One does not need to read the line as a reference to either situation, however, to have a sense that the speaker considers himself at the mercy of a group of "judges," and, for that reason, feels hostility toward them.

In the next quatrain, the issue of parent–child relations hinted at two quatrains earlier is explicitly raised. "Father" makes a stipulation for granting a simple request. As in the relationship of patients to doctors, the child's uneasy dependency on parents is connected with the diminishment of personal autonomy. The child sees him/herself in the position of double supplicant, begging the "dear linden" tree for "one of [its] leaves" so that the father will be persuaded to bring nourishment (water). The four quatrains cited above include various shifts in feeling tone, along with disruptions of narrative. Tones of empathy, mistrust, defiance (or, perhaps more accurately, a counterauthoritarian attitude), "aggressive contrition," sarcasm, and humble supplication are all presented.

Close to the issue of individual autonomy and authority is the theme of erotic attraction, which comes to the fore in much of "The Devil's Trill Sonata," especially in some of the most imaginative stanzas of the first part:

> There we are, like two crystals grown together
> In a specific rational manner, twin city in full night
> With set arias and binoculars adapted for use at the opera,
> And you so silky stretched over and under me like a steel frame.
>
> In the dim light, a romantic mollusk closes his shells
> And the bodily process suggests a lid. Ophelia green
>   like so many mottled rocks
> Drifts with her kin in an area without trees:
> Two pages face one another in a book. . . .
>
> In July we broke like strings, swimming in sea lettuce.
> And now like specimens too old to be allowed to dry
> Before mounting, merely floated onto the business paper
> To which we will finally fasten ourselves and adhere,
>   under pressure
>
> Like brown shoelaces, growing in bed or in the garden
> Common as stones and shells, held erect by the air
> And reaching you by summer and there rot, not easily seen.
> When you died, a harmless bird was permitted to
>   disappear from our sky.

In the first quatrain above, the poet places three "packed" metaphors in apposition to one another in order to depict erotic closeness. The notion of "rationality" in the "growing together" of the two clumped "crystals" seems ironic, since the crystals' particular points of juncture would happen fortuitously and the union of two lovers is generally emotionally determined. Nevertheless, the metaphor strikingly conveys the blurring (and even dissolution) of individual boundaries, like the trope of the "twin city," whose central division is apparently obscured by "full night" and complicated by placement in an operatic context. Their powerful attraction is refigured when a gentle flexibility is ascribed to the "silky" woman, who is said to cover all sides of the "steel" man's "frame."

In the third quatrain, the speaker shifts to observe a kind of enclosure in the self, "a romantic mollusk" putting a "lid" on himself. Perhaps the adjective attached to the mollusk is intended to parody masturbation as pseudoromantic or to include the desire for a transcendent self-absorption among the varieties of romantic quest. Following this image, the poet strangely recounts the suicide or drowning of the maddened Ophelia in *Hamlet*. Because of the emotional distance imposed by her lover, Hamlet, and his tragic situation, Ophelia, deathly "green like so many mottled rocks," communes with the water and its willows ("her kin"). This deadly unification is compared to a fact that metaphorically links the textual ("two pages") and the sexual.

Several quatrains later, after the "you" who seems to be assigned the role of the beloved has "brought" herself "into water, into darkness, into quiet water," as Ophelia did, the speaker/lover offers a surreal, aquatic account of what could be the disintegration of their passion: "In July, we broke like strings." This visual and kinesthetic trope effectively suggests that the relationship has "snapped" because of the wear and tear of psychological tension. There has been no violent explosion; the notion of the lovers as brittle "specimens too old to be allowed to dry / Before mounting," feeling the "pressure" to "adhere" to something as banal as business paper, is a suitably pathetic anticlimax to passion, as is the homely simile of "brown shoelaces" that "rot." Suddenly, though, the mini-"elegy" to the relationship is concluded with an especially long line in a more elevated, romantic tone. Perhaps the "harmless bird" has died *in his mind* and not in actuality, since so much of the language of this part of the poem is metaphorical. The significance of the bird's disappearance "from *our* [the lovers'?] sky" is not specified: Does the bird stand for the beloved or is it a trope of freedom that is lost to the speaker when their love is sundered?

At various points in "The Devil's Trill Sonata," the theme of eros returns. Sometimes, as in "The Cures of Love" and "The Night Sky," cited earlier, there are tropes of surreal violence: "I said, Do give me a kiss, whatever may happen. / You dusted off my coat. I hit you with a million dollars worth of mislaid gold." Amid gentler tones, we find a nightmarish, exhibitionistic, and masochistic parody of motherhood that emphasizes television's deliberate "milking" of the representation of sexuality:

> A woman showed her nipples on TV
> And inserted a syringe injecting milk
> Into her slightly swinging breasts.
> And a lovelier woman bent her head to suck.

This is a far cry from the tender line, three quatrains earlier, "I remember you when every tree was filled with you," and the airy line, twelve quatrains later, "We floated on the bed like crystal madness."

While Shapiro presents a maximal array of tropes about erotic unification, perturbation, and disintegration, he has simultaneously deleted even the representation of "solid" hints of a factual narration of the relationship. Though he refers abstractly and jocularly to the "textual" origin of passion, "Then the sentence where we met, prepared for whatever might happen like the pavement," specifics are so fractured or strangely "metaphorized" that no chance for coherent reconstruction exists. In this strategy of deletion, the erotic sections of "The Devil's Trill Sonata" resemble the elegantly fractured erotic narratives of John Ashbery's long poem, "Fragment," which displays more of an interest in the idea of isolating "the kernel of / Our [lover's] imbalance"[5] (and yet distancing oneself from it) than in the idea of "recapturing" the factual elements of what has been lost or the simplicities of "direct" emotional expression. As he made abundantly clear in my unpublished interview with him, Shapiro is "against the idea that poetry is an 'ouch,' an ejaculation, a cry of pain, a shriek of the addresser."

Soon after announcing, seemingly to the beloved (and in an echo of Shapiro's previous long poem, "About This Course"), "Next week I shall sail down on toy boats with physicists / Going as far as physicists can go, looking for you," the speaker introduces farther explorations and playfully conjures some of the special features of extraterrestrial beings. "Those of Mercury," for instance, "object to the expression of ideas by voice. / Too material, and they have a language of the eye." These mercurial beings represent the dissatisfaction with the inevitable mediations of language, the barriers to "full presence," and exemplify the desire for a "supreme fiction" of immediacy and immanence of communication. In keeping with the usual associations of the word "saturnine," "Saturnians are tormented by depression," and denizens of Venus are divided into three distinct groups:

> Venusians are gigantic but gaga and live by robbery.
> Part of Venus, however, is inhabited
>
> By beings of great gentleness, like you and me
> Who live, loving, wrong to set foot on the earth.
> Part of Venus, however, is inhabited
> By those with remarkable red lips and brown eyebrows and the
>   diaphanous joints of a crab:
>
> Light brown at the heart, shaded to green,
>   and cut into many delicate teeth.

As in the tropes of Shakespeare's *Othello*, one aspect of Venus—goddess of love (and the city of Venice)—is a lust linked with the desire for domination, while "great gentleness" and nobility in love, beyond the capacities of most earthlings, comprise another aspect. The third and wildest side of Venus is a source of visual astonishment with its representatives' bold colors, "the diaphanous joints of a crab," as well as the "many delicate teeth."

Nearly a page later, after a variety of disparate images, including musical ones, the poem's first part ends with an ominous image of separation and refusal:

> You had taken a small sip of a continuous flow
> Like a hobby a child pretends to hide
> Locking doors and resting after a squabble seemed to sever forever
> Relations, as a ship suspected of carrying disease
>   is forbidden the shore.

We cannot know for certain whether the addressee here is the poet's self, a lover, a parent, a sibling, or the reader, but let us first suppose that it is the reader. Thus, in the first line of the quatrain, the poet, through his speaker, may be teasing the reader by calling the substantial array of disjunctions that have preceded "a small sip"—more in relation to the overwhelming flux of human experience in a given day or week than to the poem as a whole, (since Part I occupies over half of the text). Even if the poem's form imitates "the continuous flow" of experience, Shapiro knows that it can only replicate a fraction of its complexity and only in a relatively short space and short (reading) time. The simile that follows can be said to compare the reading process to the "hobby" that a child uses as a partly secret refuge from stormy relations with other people. These others are suspected of having a contaminating or otherwise dangerous influence, as in the concluding simile of the "ship suspected of carrying disease is forbidden the shore."

To speculate about only one other referent for the "you," let us imagine that it is the figure of the poet (not the "literal" David Shapiro), who uses poetry to recover from different interactions. To go farther, the "squabble" which "seemed to sever forever / Relations" can be taken as the poet's "severing" of the relations between collage-element and an overarching context, or, locally, between signifier and signified. This can be read as the poet's argument against the efforts of readers to impose a coercively coherent narrative structure on "the continuous flow" with its many disjunctions or to demand such a structure from a work. However, we must note that the "squabble *seemed* to sever forever / Relations"; there is always the possibility in the rest of the poem that various forms of rapprochement will be considered and that "a ship" will no longer be "suspected of carrying disease" and will be allowed to come ashore.

Part II of "The Devil's Trill Sonata" is considerably shorter than the other two parts; it consists of fifteen quatrains. The section is full of natural imagery, but "nature" deranged by the collaging of fractured, *surreal* narratives:

Under a quarrelsome tree of blue sky
We were flying seventeen miles an hour among the poplars
Phyllis is dead and we keep hearing summer songs
while others are prostrate in weeds in snow.

This moment is gone forever
Like a snowflake on a river
And for emergency mattresses

Man uses Spanish moss. . . .

That night the oak tree was rather blunt
Not a fast grower
It had lived six hundred years
Winky the Dog was snarling back at David

In the first quatrain above, the poet presents a bizarre, contradictory multienvironment in which the unspecified "we" are simultaneously positioned under a tree—not one composed of wood and leaves but a "quarrelsome" one "of blue sky," like an image of reversal in the surreal painting of Magritte—and yet "flying seventeen miles an hour among the poplars." In addition, their hearing "summer songs" is presented concurrently with "others" being "prostrate in weeds in snow" and the announcement that a named but otherwise unidentified woman is "dead." As in the later "Commentary Text Commentary Text Commentary Text," discussed in chapter 1, and in numerous other short poems by Shapiro, a literal "deterritorialization" occurs. It would be futile to search for ways in which the oppositions of stasis/motion and summer/winter can be reconciled in one coherent "picture." The poet's derangement of the "common-sense" (sensory) description of temporal and spatial unities (or units) is established as an alternative to imagistic poems that merely record these unities, as though such language can tell "the whole story" and is not founded on somewhat arbitrary inclusions and exclusions.

Rather than affirming pastoral pleasantries, the poet emphasizes the condition of transcience and what Ashbery calls "fundamental absences"[6] in a rhyming couplet: "This moment is gone forever / Like a snowflake on a river." In these lines, Shapiro deliberately seems to reverse the idealism of Shelley while echoing the British Romantic poet. In "Prometheus Unbound," "Asia" says of its soul: "It seems to float ever, forever / Upon that many-winding river."[7] In "Ode to Liberty," Shelley writes: "Within the surface of Time's fleeting river / Its wrinkled image lies, as then it lay / Immovably unquiet," and yet unable to "pass away!"[8] Apart from their striking negation of Shelley's tropes of eternity, the doubling effect in Shapiro's words indicate how poetic language can shake up stabilities: While "this moment" can be said to refer primarily to a particular instant of perception, it can also be read self-referentially as a contradiction of its own premise. The "immortality" of the written word "preserves" "this moment" of poetic utterance for as long as the book, *Lateness,* exists materially.

Swiftly shifting to a statement about the improvised use of mossy "mattresses" in the wilderness, the poet suggests that the disquieting awareness of transcience includes an adaptation, a willingness to make do with transient materials. On the other hand, the next quatrain challenges the scope of this aura of generalization by showing that some elements in nature—the six-hundred year old oak tree, for instance—are not so easily perceived according to a typical human understanding of transience, although they, too, will die. In turn, the oak's "loftiness" is undercut by the trivial domesticity of the next observation about a "dog." Directly after the startling image of "a violin in blue white fire," the last two quatrains of Part II mingle a sense of the precariousness of existence, erotic vulnerability, and a desperate desire to escape death through erotic intensity:

You have not touched me,
but the injury is as great.
It may be we do not have enough October, November, December.
There is another approach:

Kissed in daringness.
Looked for nearby sea.
Yet to pass beneath these misted trees seems not enough.
Laughing at death as you forget the dream.

Although the opening reproach has a lucid simplicity, the reference to touch is teasingly ambiguous. Has the other person refrained from physically wounding the speaker and yet injured him psychologically, or has she refrained from touching him sexually and thus has disturbed his psyche? In either case, although the speaker—if it is the same speaker, and we can never be sure—had stated a quatrain earlier, "I ordered you to judge me fairly," he is painfully vulnerable to erotic judgment. As an assessment of how much time is left to assuage the relationship's "injuries," the listing of the *last* three months of the year—as opposed to the *January* which signaled Shapiro's poetic debut—may have an apocalyptic ring, either personal or collective. The months evoke what Frank Kermode calls "the sense of an ending."

Aside from the contemplation of mortality and the calculation of remaining time, the other "approach" is a "daring" stab at passion. But note that "There is another approach" is placed in the present tense, while "kissed in daringness" is either placed in the past tense *or* referring to the reception of a kiss. The truncated syntax does not permit one to choose between these two readings: the approach is either a retreat to the past, which can be viewed as futile nostalgia, or a surrender to the present and a forgetting of past and future. Similarly, the fragment, "Looked for nearby sea," indicates a past effort or the notion that the sea is "looked for" by someone. The next line, however, states that the movement to water, mentioned in different contexts several times earlier in the poem "seems not enough." For the moment, the addressee chooses to "laugh at death" as she "forget[s] the dream." "Dream," the last word of Part II, might signify the plan for escape (thus implying that the woman, facing the inevitability of death, laughs cathartically instead of remembering the plan) or it might signify a frightening nocturnal image or even a premonition of death that laughter temporarily displaces in the woman's consciousness. Thus, closure in this part of the poem does not shut down interpretation but reopens it.

Toward the beginning of Part III of "The Devil's Trill Sonata," Ophelia, having made a brief appearance in the first section, is reintroduced:

Ophelia preferred to be silk
Rather than inside the glass
The first car hits the second, the second the third,
        and so on
Each whirlpool produces a dimple for Hamlet

Ophelia is some sort of fluid
The silk cloth is rubbed and she flows
Her comparatively small body wades into the stream
She has been rubbed off and migrates into the silk

You make a rough sketch of the swordplay
And the sword tilts
Hamlet drifts like water through the pipes
The earth is a magnet that can be switched on or off,
        but where is that switch?

The opening line of this passage recalls the line, "and you so silky stretched over and under me like a steel frame," in the first section. Ophelia, however, is not perceived as a "covering" here; she assumes a fluid, silken state in lieu of accepting a highly restrictive form of protection from the elements ("rather than inside the glass"). Perhaps pertaining to the chain of causes and effects resulting in many gruesome deaths in Shakespeare's tragedy, a domino effect of cars is presented next. The speaker then links the cars' collision to "whirpools," each of which "produces a dimple for Hamlet," or, instead, may be suggesting that Ophelia's sinking into a watery grave had created the whirpools "for" her estranged beloved. The bizarre trivialization of Ophelia's self-sacrifice and Hamlet's quest is followed by a further elaboration of the trope of the young woman's "fluidity." Idealized imagery of flow bumps harshly against the cold, awkward observation about her "wading," and the vulgar aspect of the double meaning of "rubbed off" perturbs the romantic notion that she "migrates into the silk"—"silk" signifying water—in order to become one with that primal element.

In the next quatrain, Hamlet, too, is linked with water, drifting "through the pipes." The speaker may be pointing to the suppleness and fluidity—not necessarily "indecisiveness," as some critics have said—of his thinking, as he moves through the maze of his situation toward the goal of revenge. The question in the next line seeks a first cause for the earth's operations; perhaps it serves as a gentle parody of Hamlet's pained, metaphysical meditations in some of the soliloquies. The idea of "that switch" is a supreme fiction, on which the poet refuses to fixate. Such refusals of whatever impedes multiplicity are aptly characterized, two pages later, by the lines: "There are no rules / But there are many songs / Easily heard by putting your ear to the window." (Songs, of course, have *provisional* rules, just as "The Devil's Trill Sonata" is divided into quatrains.) Obviously, the author of the poem has put his ear to many "windows" in collaging a multitude of conflicting "songs" of many "characters."

If "that switch" to the magnetized earth is unavailable to the earnest quester, there is always the possibility of using imagination and technology to reverse fundamental perceptions of cause and effect, as in the cinematic effects of the Russian, Vertov:

> We can imagine a film run backwards
> Pure milk leaps into the jug
> The ashes form a new log
> The omelet reconverts into the chicken
>
> The wind which reduces the snowy comedienne
>   to a hat
> But the hat flies back to the store
> The ancient city is frost
> And rubble rebuilds in a show of heat
>
> The film didn't deceive you for too long
> You saw the joke reforming
> On the face of the custard pie
> I am of no further use to you

This sprightly visual detour from the "story" of Ophelia and Hamlet charts the flux of movement from states of dissemination or decomposition to those of prior wholeness and thus spawns an "arresting" fiction of the undoing of mortality, a stunning return to beginnings. In the image of "the omelet" reconverting "into the chicken," several crucial steps are humorously left out! The fiction is sapped of power when its structure is apprehended; the "deception" becomes apparent with repetition of the process ("the joke reforming"). The "I" who is "of no further use" may signify the narrator and, by extension, the fiction itself, as though it could self-deprecatingly announce its own departure. Of course, the puncturing of an "uplifting" experience can prove disorienting: "The balloon's buoyant joke is punctured and snow fills the whole room with disordered clothes." At various points in the poem, snow is used as a disruptive force. After the cinematic joke has been "punctured," Ophelia returns (for the last time):

> Lumps of clay collide
> And the photograph of Ophelia trails a small bubble
> Ophelia still unspent at the end of time
> The fountain spouts downward
>
> It was that small fictional dog
> That eventually brought us down into the sand

> There is only one real Hamlet, but the student
>   is advised not to adopt it
> Ophelia, there is only one true Ophelia
>
> She hangs from her string
> And the pilot cuts it

Fragmentarily, the speaker seems to describe some sort of planetary upheaval, apparently "at the end of time." "Lumps of clay collide" and "the fountain spouts downward," as though the earth's gravity had been madly scrambled. "Ophelia" remains "unspent at the end of time" in the sense that a trace of her endures, a metaphorical "photograph" of a fictional being who, of course, could never have been photographed.

Ophelia's "immortality"—her transcendence of the fate of death by drowning—is achieved through readers and writers continually "re-vising" her and other characters in *Hamlet*. For example, Rimbaud reanimates the scene of her death in the romantic poem that bears her name; Eliot can be said to bring together aspects of Hamlet and Polonius—along with the concluding image of drowning—in "The Love-Song of J. Alfred Prufrock"; Pasternak articulates how Hamlet "stands alone" in his poem of that name; and Brecht offers his own dramatic revision of Shakespeare's play.

The notions that "There is only one real Hamlet," which "the student is" offhandedly but seriously "advised not to adopt," and that "there is only one true Ophelia" are immediately recognizable as hollow fictions. In the literary and historical allusions of the poem, Shapiro supplements revisions of fictional traces with further revisions. The "real" and "true" characters exist, but only as concepts whose concrete manifestations are absent. One final time, the poem represents Ophelia's "final" plunge: "the pilot" assumes the position of one of the Three Fates in cutting Ophelia's string.

Like Ashbery in "The Skaters" and elsewhere, Shapiro concretely represents his theme of deletion. Three-and-one-half pages after the cutting of Ophelia's string, the speaker gives instructions for performing an act of erasure. Whimsically mentioning the "presence" of "Eaton's Berkshire Typewriter Paper A 201 and liquid eraser fluid," he states—in three of the poem's shortest lines: "Shake well, touch on / Blow for instant dry / Retype. Product penetrates." Since deletion is followed by rewriting itself and is a kind of rewriting, the text, as in the closing lines of "To an Idea," can be considered a palimpsest; erasures are materially present alongside collaged accretions. Much history, however, is lost beneath these erasures; sometimes the "product penetrates" too sharply. In "Definition of Blue," Ashbery admires the "smooth" surface of a palimpsest developed from "diversions" and "multiple corrections" while cautioning that the "portrait" that results "has no relation to the space or time in which it was lived."[9]

Following the instructions for using "liquid eraser fluid," there is a lurid, ironic reference to a deletion that profoundly affected American political life, the assassination of President John Kennedy:

> But the specific achievement of America
> Expressed in the scar above the temple
> In which the bullet is painted, in blonde hair,
> Is the unsparing "trans-naturalism," blending both head and bullet

"The unsparing 'trans-naturalism'" evidently involves the ascendancy of murderous violence, which the "blending" of "both head and bullet" in a rendering of the slain president is said to exemplify and which the speaker sarcastically labels America's "specific achievement." This focus on pernicious deletion, conveyed unemotionally, as the norm of political life probably marks Shapiro's disgust, not only at the assassination of the two Kennedys and of Martin Luther King, but at what he perceived then as the failure of the "new left" movement of the late 1960s to effect broad social change.

In addition, the deletions of the Nixon administration in the Watergate scandal were being exposed on national television and in the newspapers while he was writing the poem. In Part I, there had been an allusion to the coverup: "It's as if . . . / my throat were being torn by a crying gibbon / Whose voice could be heard throughout Washington / Crying, Liar! Liar! I have something to say to you all! / Come to the eastern mirage-tower at once!" In Part III, such "erasure" must be performed meticulously and repeatedly: "Time for a second coat, where the white ink smeared / Non-toxic and nonflammable / The squat figures of Senators groping for work." (Of course, Nixon's authorized deletions of incriminating tapes became highly "flammable.") The image of "the squat figures of Senators"—perhaps a reading of the "rorschach" produced by the "second coat" of eraser fluid—may underscore the notion of much institutional political activity (busywork) as an erasure of possibility, a stultifying negation, amid the necessity, at that time, for legislators to expose the crimes of the president and some of his followers with dispatch.

The concluding quatrains of "The Devil's Trill Sonata" begin with the image of a kaleidoscope, highly appropriate for a poem that affirms multiplicity, and then move to a rapid collaging of disparate elements:

> It's nice to have a kaleidoscope in the house.
> You stamp your foot in the lagoon, you can't even cross
>   the same river once.
> Wading placidly and alive, you enjoy your borrowed toys.
> You walk out for the Sunday Times and forget to return.
>
> The sun rises above the pitcher's mound, like a mail boat
> The stars are now thoroughly scotch-taped
>   along the sky
> And we lie together like tree-lined streets
> The speed-limit sign and the white Volkswagen
>
> The Divine Comedy of a postcard
> Living on the earth is like dinner on the ground
> The air is filled with warm air and torn pocketbooks
> THE President has some other good news:
>
> The sky is blank because it's blue
> The sky is blank and it is blue, filled with habits,
>   filled with habitable houses
> Filled with spirits
> "But I don't see anything"
>
> It's a bright day in the mail boat
> The sun keeps rising out of the mist, large
>   and calm
> The wind passes the pump house
> As if it entertained great scorn of Hell

After the introduction of the "kaleidoscope" in the poem's "house," Heraclitus's aforementioned version of multiplicity is revised and rendered even more "multiple": Any "single" experience is split into a heterogeneity. "The lagoon" is a fluid multiplicity. "You can't even cross the same river once," since the river's components are "de-territorialized" and "reterritorialized" throughout one's crossing. As in previous (sometimes less positive) references to childhood in the poem, all "toys" are "borrowed," just as one's existence is.

The next quatrain features allusions to Fairfield Porter's paintings, "The Sun Rising" and "Tree-Lined Streets." In Porter's work, hints of quasi-expressionistic paint-handling and unusual perspectives make suburban domestic scenes suddenly worthy of fresh attention, just as Shapiro's collages sometimes shed a fresh light on domestic images. Simultaneously, there is an evocation of nostalgia and an implicit critique of the domination of surfaces. One way to make sense of the bizarre comparison of "the sun" rising "above the pitcher's mound" and "a mail boat" would be to imagine or recall the boat rendered in Porter's painting from a perspective that makes it seem to rise from the water. Another, more tenuous, connection would be that the sun "communicates" light and the boat makes possible the communication occurring through mail.

As in the celestial coda of Ashbery's "The Skaters" and in some of Cornell's box-sculptures, the makeshift collaging of fragments announces itself as a replacement for the vain dream of a totalizing image. Earlier in Part III, the poet had referred to "the whole surface thus scotch-taped" and here he asserts: "The stars are now thoroughly scotch-taped along the sky." When lovers "lie together"—note the pun in the verb—"like tree-lined streets / The speed-limit sign and the white Volkswagen," a limiting, insular homogeneity within the vast, unruly heterocosm is chided.

In the century of what Walter Benjamin called "the age of mechanical reproduction," the grand, allegorical structure of Dante's "Divine Comedy" is shrunk to the confines of a "postcard," but in this pseudo-process, the power of the "original" work and its epic effects are absurdly diminished. A general debasement ("Living on the earth is like dinner on the ground" rather than Manet's "luncheon on the grass") and a precarious economic climate ("The air is filled with . . . torn pocketbooks") are evoked.

As for the president's "other good news," it strangely continues the other report about the sky, with its "blankness" and "blueness." It also recalls President Richard Nixon's imposition of crucial "blanks" or gaps in "news" about the workings of government during his 1972 re-election campaign, thus allowing Nixon to evade aspects of his accountability to those who elected him. Next, we learn that the sky is "filled with habits, filled with habitable houses / Filled with spirits." In these lines of Stevensian repetition, the pun on "habits" underscores the habitual perceptions that make the sky "blank"—that is, untransformed by a fresh imagination—and the (possibly opposing) notion that the sky is filled with "clothing." One can choose to make the "blank" and "blue" sky a suburb populated by suburban "spirits," just as Nixon spoke of a "silent majority" of Americans who allegedly supported his aims. On the other hand, the "spirits" in the sky may also signify the "ghosts"—or, if you will, the "skeletons in his closet"—that would eventually strip Nixon of his presidential power. A more "blank" response challenges the assertions of "vision": "'But I don't see anything.'" Of course, this lack of sight in others is precisely what a cover-up like that in Nixon's administration is intended to produce.

In the poem's closing quatrain, "the President" is set aside, and the motifs of "mail boat" and sun return. The trope of communication seems intentionally banalized by an artificial cheeriness. The "bright day" and the multiple repetition of the sunrise could be a sign of hope and clarification, but it might also indicate how one's perception of the sun and the environment in general can be drained of intensity. Next, a source of vital energy, "the wind," shoots *past* the point at which it can be harnessed fruitfully. Wind seems to be viewed as a hellish and not a life-enhancing force, as evidenced by the citation of a line translated from Dante's *Inferno*: "As if it entertained great scorn of Hell." Should the reader conclude from this ominous ending that the entire poem must be read in a pessimistic light? To draw such a conclusion would be to cast aside the understanding of multiplicity, in which endings are pseudo-endings (or, at best, provisional resting points), just as beginnings are merely provisional and do not signify a privileged "origin" of discourse.

For the sake of practicality, this long string or stream of collages had to conclude at some point. In addition, one can attach as much significance to the first words of the last line, "As if" (with their underscoring of how tropes involve a "turning" from one element to another), as on the last word, "Hell." The notion of "entertaining" (considering) "great scorn of Hell" is a far cry from the condition of embracing or fully internalizing a hellish state. A "quantitative" analysis of the poem's emotional "terrain" might yield a greater degree of lament and negative critique in "The Devil's Trill Sonata" than celebration and affirmation or a more neutral tone. But this "kaleidoscopic" poem is marked most saliently by the *diversity* of its attitudes. This diversity thwarts the assumption that the poem "settles" upon any particular emotional ground: "A baby held on to a car / I said, Little baby, do you know where you are / One moment in Italy, the next moment in Greece."

"The Devil's Trill Sonata" brings various aspects of Shapiro's shorter work into a single poetic "field." While the sustained critique of modes of representation in many poems of the 1980s is not to be found here, the poet does include fragmentary depositions of attempts at totalization. Although the collage-elements that dominate "The Devil's Trill Sonata" are somewhat more open to thematic interpretation than the extreme experimental dislocations of "The Heavenly Humor," "Poems from Deal," and similar short poems, an "atmosphere" of disjunction still prevails over any attempt to reduce the multiplicity of the whole poem or one of its sections to a unity. (As I have tried to indicate, instances of discursivity are far from absent; they sometimes appear "out of left field.") Finally, Shapiro's longest poem includes diverse treatments of erotic themes that parallel the achievements of such poems as "An Exercise in Futility," "A Song," and "You Are Tall and Thin."

Often seducing his readers with intriguing hints of palpability—"And we moved along the path dazzled by ice on mica"—and allowing them again and again to break out of determinate contexts into fascinatingly unfamiliar areas—"Your brain like a tennis ball somewhere in the stands"—Shapiro in his grand "Sonata" keeps rewarding them with plural pleasures and keeps them wildly off balance.

Conclusion

Before offering some concluding remarks about the value of David Shapiro's poetry, I must ask how readers of poetry can or should go about the business of assessing value.

In recent years, the possibility of making overall judgments of literary value has been called into question. The urgency of multicultural canon reformation (and the questioning of the entire concept of a "canon") in literary studies, the widespread skepticism about absolute notions of "Truth" and "Value," and the concomitant desire for the development of multiperspectival understandings make it seem slightly absurd to pose the question, "Who are the best contemporary American poets?"

Understanding that one probably cannot hope for more than a thoroughly described subjectivity (and at times what can be called an "intersubjectivity"), I would like to propose that a different, slightly less general question should be put in its place: With respect to a specific and precisely delineated *context*, which current American poets produce work that raises the most significant and interesting questions and/or formulations in the most cogent ways? The use of such a question helps to rule out dangerous and reductive arguments that try to establish one context as so significant that all others are of negligible importance.

I am aware of the limitations of the term "context" as a spatial metaphor. Contexts can be said to "enclose," be "enclosed by," and interpenetrate each other; to separate them involves an arbitrary act of will. However, the use of "context" in question enables both the production of thought about value and the avoidance of coercively exclusivist, antipluralistic thinking. Among the readers of contemporary poetry, some place greatest importance on the general context of power relations; within this group, some are most concerned with issues of gender, others with those of race, others with class, and still others with the configurations of multinational capitalism. Some readers might value contemporary poetry insofar as it illuminates and/or is illuminated by a variety of psychological theories or even some pretheoretical notion of the "experience" of human interaction. While appreciating the impingement of political, sociological, and psychological contexts on poetry, others may focus chiefly on particular questions of aesthetic achievement, including the "freshness" of the use of tropes, sensory imagery, meter, rhythm, etc. Other readers might study poetry for the particular ways in which it comments on metaphysical and epistemological questions. Among these readers are those who value in poetry an elucidation of the problematics of language as representation.

It is reasonable to expect that one who is devoted to the study of literature may be interested (to greater and lesser degrees) in all of these contexts and in their interactions, for example, in the politics of aesthetic form and the aestheticization of power relations. However, it is *unreasonable* to expect that a given poet (or critic, for that matter) can or should powerfully address all or most of these contexts in her/his work in order to be considered "worth reading." The myth of Dante or Shakespeare as authors whose work "encompasses" every aspect of human experience has, I hope, been laid to rest. Depending on which context or group of them a literary critic wishes to explore at a given time, s/he will select different authors or groups of authors for analysis. Such obvious points are made here only to guard against the totalitarian and totalizing uses sometimes made of such clichés as "Everything is political."

In his mature poetry of the 1970s and 1980s, David Shapiro, I believe, has earned a place among twentieth-century American poets like Stevens and Ashbery, whose poetic speculations on representation have provoked numerous readers' serious and complex reflection. In this context, he is at the forefront of his generation of poets. Although Shapiro is a poet in mid-career, it is not premature to make this judgment, because the highly accomplished "Devil's Trill Sonata" was completed when the poet was only twenty-seven, and in his third decade, he wrote an impressive number of deeply engaging poems. Note also that *To an Idea*, his sixth book, was published when Shapiro was thirty-six, whereas Stevens's first book, *Harmonium*, appeared when he was forty.

Recently, some American critics have been claiming that various "Language Poets" like Charles Bernstein, Susan Howe, Ron Silliman, Bruce Andrews, and Michael Palmer are the contemporaries who have the most to offer in the context under discussion. Thus far, I have found the theoretical prose pronouncements of members of this loosely knit group much more compelling than most of the poetry, much of which appears to be less musically acute examples of the kind of disjunctive collaging that Shapiro was doing a good deal earlier—in the 1960s and early 1970s—and which I characterized in chapter 1. The most interesting, if not yet thoroughly persuasive, aspect of "language" theorizing is the critique of narrative and other forms of referential functioning as an intentionally political act.

Scholarship on the actual poetry of these writers is relatively new; critics' accounts have done little thus far to make me question this impression. (Many "Language Poets" find the distinction between theoretical prose and poetry mystified; I would respond that making distinctions in aesthetic form does not necessarily impose a hierarchy that places poetry "above" theoretical prose.)

While Shapiro's aesthetic accomplishments are considerable, what makes his poetry, in my view, deserve extensive study are the ways in which the critical or theoretical element is deployed. The "Language Poets" rely heavily on disjunction; sometimes, this can be intriguing, but at other times, the theoretical force of the intentions seems blunted by the sense that juxtapositions are merely arbitrary. In other cases, "Language Poets'" discursive critique or representation of representation seems too obvious, simplistic, or else promising but cursory. These impressions are tentative; I hope that future criticism details points of relation and difference between Shapiro and various "Language Poets." In order for critics to do this, they had better recognize Shapiro's powerful achievements in the context that the "Language Poets" have identified as their own.

My contention that Shapiro is one of the most accomplished twentieth-century American poets in the context of the analysis and critique of representation is founded on various close readings I have attempted, especially those in chapter 2. As Shapiro has, many poets of this century have made assertions in their work about the failure or insufficiency of "supreme fictions" to recover origins, or fixed, absolute "Truth," or phenomenological immanence in language. These findings or lessons in and of themselves do not make a poet's work valuable; they can also be found in innumerable philosophical, sociological, psychological, and other texts. Value can be determined by how interestingly, persuasively, and vibrantly the thought (some might say *language*) processes leading up to these findings and the findings themselves are enacted or "performed" in poetry. The poet's awareness of and intervention in the process of reading itself is also a crucial part of this performance.

In reading Shapiro's poetry, I have found again and again that the most outstanding feature has been the complex, unpredictable enactment of mediation (or, to use very "material" spatial metaphors, layering or palimpsest) in the experience of interpretation and perception in general. Shapiro's complex tropes, bursting with polysemy and the repeated crossing and uncrossing of binary oppositions, his startling disjunctive trajectories which evocatively map multiple disclosures and concealments, and his peculiar and yet precise uses of abstraction, including "meta"-commentary about the acts of reading and writing, exhort the reader to think through the problematics of representation and desire energetically, sensuously, and rigorously.

Notes

Introduction

1. Quotations from *A Man Holding an Acoustic Panel* are cited in the text using the following abbrevation; when lines are sufficiently located, no citation appears:

    MHAP: David Shapiro, *A Man Holding an Acoustic Panel* (New York: E. P. Dutton, 1971).

2. Quotations from *House (Blown Apart)* are cited in the text using the following abbreviation; when lines are sufficiently located, no citation appears:

    HBA: David Shapiro, *House (Blown Apart)* (Woodstock, N.Y.: Overlook Press, 1988).

3. Quotations from *To an Idea* are cited in the text using the following abbreviation; when lines are sufficiently located, no citation appears:

    TI: David Shapiro, *To an Idea* (Woodstock, N.Y.: Overlook Press, 1983)

4. Jorie Graham, "Three Poets Wondering Who They Are," *New York Times Book Review* (4 March 1984): 14.
5. Barbara Johnson, *The Critical Difference* (Baltimore, Md.: Johns Hopkins University Press, 1980), xi–xii.
6. Quotations from *John Ashbery: An Introduction to the Poetry* are cited in the text using the following abbreviation; when lines are sufficiently located, no citation appears:

    JA: David Shapiro, *John Ashbery: An Introduction to the Poetry* (New York: Columbia University Press, 1979).

7. Stephen Paul Miller, "Jasper Johns and David Shapiro, an Analogy" (Master's thesis, City College of New York, 1983), 19.
8. Quotations from *The Page-Turner* are cited in the text using the following abbreviation; when lines are sufficiently located, no citation appears:

    PT: David Shapiro, *The Page-Turner* (New York: Liveright, 1973).

9. Quotations from *January* are cited in the text using the following abbreviation; when lines are sufficiently located, no citation appears:

       J: David Shapiro, *January* (New York: Holt, Rinehart and Winston, 1965).

10. Stephen Paul Miller, "Jasper Johns and David Shapiro, an Analogy," 36.
11. "Where Are They Now?" *Newsweek* (13 October 1969): 45.
12. Ibid.
13. "Cynical Idealists of '68," *Time* (7 June 1968): 82–83.
14. Quotations from *Poems from Deal* are cited in the text using the following abbreviation; when lines are sufficiently located, no citation appears:

       PD: David Shapiro, *Poems from Deal* (New York: E. P. Dutton, 1969).

15. "Keeping a Sense of Commitment," *Time* (19 May 1986): 43.
16. John Koethe, "Freely Espoused," *Poetry*, 117 (October 1970): 56.
17. David Shapiro, *Jasper Johns Drawings 1954–1984*. (New York: Abrams, 1984), 11.
18. Jerome J. McGann, "The Importance of Being Ordinary," *Poetry*, 125 (October 1974): 51.
19. Quotations from *Lateness*, which is unpaginated, are cited in the text using the following abbreviation; when lines are sufficiently located, no citation appears:

       L: David Shapiro, *Lateness* (Woodstock, N.Y.: Overlook Press, 1977).

Chapter 1. Thresholds of Readability: The Disjunctive Collage-Poems

1. David Shapiro, *Poets and Painters: Lines of Color* (Denver: Denver Art Museum, 1981), 10–11.

Chapter 2. Desire, Representation, and Critique

1. Wallace Stevens, *The Collected Poems* (New York: Knopf, 1977), 176.
2. Ibid., 486.
3. Paul A. Bové, *Destructive Poetics: Heidegger and Modern American Poetry* (New York: Columbia University Press, 1980), 187.
4. Stevens, *The Collected Poems*, 381.
5. Ibid.
6. Ibid., 382.
7. Frank O'Hara, "Personism: a Manifesto," in *The Poetics of the New American Poetry*, Donald M. Allen and Warren Tallman, eds. (New York: Grove Press, 1973), 355.
8. Stevens, *The Collected Poems*, 397.
9. John Ashbery, *Self-Portrait in a Convex Mirror* (New York: Viking Press, 1975), 7.
10. Shapiro, *Jasper Johns Drawings 1954–1984*, 14.
11. David Shapiro, *After a Lost Original* (New York: Solo Press, 1992).
12. See Jacques Derrida, *Margins of Philosophy*, trans. Alan Bass (Chicago: the University of Chicago Press, 1982), 329–30.

13. Stevens, *The Collected Poems*, 383–84.
14. John Ashbery, *Rivers and Mountains* (New York: Holt, Rinehart and Winston, 1967), 63.

Chapter 3. "Mirrors Rushing into Each Other": The Poetics of Eros

1. Elizabeth Bishop, *The Complete Poems* (New York: Farrar, Straus and Giroux, 1978), 3.
2. Gilles Deleuze and Claire Parnet, *Dialogues*, trans. Hugh Tomlinson and Barbara Habberiam (New York: Columbia University Press, 1987), 96–97.
3. Ashbery, *Rivers and Mountains*, 56–58.
4. Shapiro, *After a Lost Original*.
5. Jean Baudrillard, *In the Shadow of the Silent Majorities . . . or the End of the Social and Other Essays*, trans. Paul Foss, Paul Patton, and John Johnston (New York: Semiotext[e], 1983), 83–84.

Chapter 4. "The Pluralism of Possible Styles": A Reading of "The Devil's Trill Sonata"

1. David Shapiro, *Jim Dine: Painting What One Is* (New York: Harry N. Abrams, 1981), 69–70.
2. T. S. Eliot, *The Complete Poems and Plays, 1909–1950* (New York: Harcourt, Brace and World, 1971), 50.
3. Shapiro, *Jim Dine: Painting What One Is*, 33.
4. Gilles Deleuze and Felix Guattari. *On the Line*, trans. John Johnson (New York: Semiotext[e], 1983), 47–49.
5. John Ashbery, *The Double Dream of Spring* (New York: E. P. Dutton, 1970), 82.
6. Ashbery, *Rivers and Mountains*, 39.
7. Percy Bysshe Shelley, *The Selected Poetry and Prose* (New York: New American Library, 1966), 175.
8. Ibid., 251.
9. Ashbery, *The Double Dream of Spring*, 53.

Bibliography

Ashbery, John. *The Tennis Court Oath*. Middletown, Conn.: Wesleyan University Press, 1962.

———. *Rivers and Mountains*. New York: Holt, Rinehart and Winston, 1967.

———. *The Double Dream of Spring*. New York: E. P. Dutton, 1970.

———. *Self-Portrait in a Convex Mirror*. New York: Viking, 1975.

Atlas, James. Review of *A Man Holding an Acoustic Panel* by David Shapiro. *Poetry* 121.10 (January 1973): 229.

Baudrillard, Jean. *In the Shadow of the Silent Majorities . . . or the End of the Social and Other Essays*. Translated by Paul Foss, Paul Patton, and John Johnston. New York: Semiotext(e), 1983.

Bishop, Elizabeth. *The Complete Poems*. New York: Farrar, Straus and Giroux, 1978.

Bloom, Harold. "The Year's Best Books in Poetry" (including review of *Lateness* by David Shapiro). *New Republic*, 26 November 1977, 26.

Bové, Paul A. *Destructive Poetics: Heidegger and Modern American Poetry*. New York: Columbia University Press, 1980.

Cohen, Arthur A. "David Shapiro." In *Contemporary Poets*, 3d ed., edited by James Vinson, 1375–76. New York: Saint Martin's, 1980.

"Cynical Idealists of '68." *Time*, 7 June 1968, 81.

Deleuze, Gilles, and Felix Guattari. *On the Line*. Translated by John Johnston. New York: Semiotext(e), 1983.

——— and Claire Parnet. *Dialogues*. Translated by Hugh Tomlinson and Barbara Habberiam. New York: Columbia University Press, 1987.

Derrida, Jacques. *Of Grammatology*. Translated by Gayatri Chakravorty Spivak. Baltimore, Md.: Johns Hopkins University Press, 1976.

———. *Margins of Philosophy*. Translated by Alan Bass. Chicago: University of Chicago Press, 1982.

Eliot, T. S. *The Complete Poems and Plays, 1909–1950*. New York: Harcourt, Brace & World, 1971.

Fink, Thomas. "The Poetry of David Shapiro and Ann Lauterbach: After Ashbery." *American Poetry Review* 17.1 (January/February 1988): 27–32.

———. Review of *"House (Blown Apart)"* by David Shapiro. *Minnesota Review* 32 (Spring 1989): 157–59.

Graham, Jorie. "Three Poets Wondering Who They Are" (including review of *To an Idea* by David Shapiro). *New York Times Book Review*, 4 March 1984, 14.

Johnson, Barbara. *The Critical Difference*. Baltimore, Md.: Johns Hopkins University Press, 1980.

"Keeping a Sense of Commitment." *Time*, 19 May 1986, 43.

Koethe, John. "Freely Espoused" (including review of *Poems from Deal* by David Shapiro). *Poetry* 17.1 (October 1970): 56–57.

Lyotard, Jean-François. *The Postmodern Condition: A Report on Knowledge.* Translated by Geoff Bennington and Brian Massumi. Minneapolis: University of Minnesota Press, 1984.

McGann, Jerome J. "The Importance of Being Ordinary" (including review of *The Page-Turner* by David Shapiro). *Poetry.* 125.1 (October 1974): 50–52.

Malanga, Gerald. "Three Firsts" (including review of *January* by David Shapiro). *Poetry* 108.2 (May 1966): 132–33.

Miller, Stephen Paul. "Jasper Johns and David Shapiro, an Analogy." Master's Thesis, City College of New York, 1983.

O'Hara, Frank. "Personism: a Manifesto." In *The Poetics of The New American Poetry*, edited by Donald M. Allen and Warren Tallman, 353–55. New York: Grove, 1973.

Shapiro, David. *January.* New York: Holt, Rinehart and Winston, 1965.

———. *Poems from Deal.* New York: E. P. Dutton, 1969.

———. "Hockney Paints a Portrait." *Art News* 68.3 (May 1969): 28–31.

———. "Strawberry Cake with the Psyche of a Good Camera." *Art News* 69.8 (December 1970): 30–31, 67–70.

———. *A Man Holding an Acoustic Panel.* New York: E. P. Dutton, 1971.

———. "Homage to Albers." *Art News* 70.7 (November 1971): 31–33, 96–97.

———. *The Page-Turner.* New York: Liveright, 1973.

———. "Eva Hesse." *Craft Horizons* 33.1 (February 1973): 40–45, 71–72.

———. "Frank O'Hara." In *Contemporary Poets*, 2d ed., edited by James Vinson, 1778–81. New York: St. Martin's Press, 1975.

———. *Lateness.* Woodstock, N.Y.: Overlook Press, 1977.

———. *Toward Stevens: The Will to Poetry.* New York: Poetry Mailing List, 1977.

———. *John Ashbery: An Introduction to the Poetry.* New York: Columbia University Press, 1979.

———. *Poets and Painters: Lines of Color.* Denver, Colo.: Denver Art Museum, 1979.

———. "On a Villanelle by Elizabeth Bishop." *Iowa Review* 10.1 (Winter 1979): 77–81.

———. *Jim Dine: Painting What One Is.* New York: Harry N. Abrams, 1981.

———. *To an Idea.* Woodstock, N.Y.: Overlook Press, 1983.

———. *Jasper Johns Drawings 1954–1984.* New York: Harry N. Abrams, 1984.

———. "Art as Collaboration: Toward a Theory of Pluralist Aesthetics." In *The Artist as Collaborator*, edited by Cynthia Jaffee McCabe, 1–28. District of Columbia: Smithsonian Institution Press, 1984.

———. *House (Blown Apart).* Woodstock, N.Y.: Overlook Press, 1988.

———. Interview with author. New York, N.Y., 20 December 1989.

———. "Domination of Blanks: Painting and Poetry's Truth." *Gregory Botts.* New York: Anne Plumb Gallery, 1989.

———. "Fury and Indestructibility: Notes after the Holocaust." In *Testimony: Contemporary Writers Make the Holocaust Personal*, edited by David Rosenberg, 456–74. New York: Times Books, 1989.

———. *Mondrian: Flowers.* New York: Harry N. Abrams, 1991.

———. After a *Lost Original.* New York: Solo Press, 1992.

Shelley, Percy Bysshe. *The Selected Poetry and Prose.* New York: New American Library, 1966.

Shetley, Vernon. "A Babel of Tongues" (including a review of *Lateness* by David Shapiro). *Poetry* 134.4 (July 1979): 231–33.

Stevens, Wallace. *The Collected Poems.* New York: Knopf, 1977.

"Where Are They Now?" *Newsweek,* 13 October 1969, 52.

Index

Aeschylus, 90
Alighieri, Dante: *The Divine Comedy*, 48, 108–9, 112
Allen, Donald: *The New American Poetry*, 17
Ashbery, John, 15, 17–18, 26, 27, 28–30, 41, 50, 51, 81, 82, 84, 112; "As You Came from the Holy Land," 55; "Definition of Blue," 106; "Europe," 88, 92; "Fragment," 97; "The Skaters," 67, 100, 105; *The Tennis Court Oath*, 37–38; *Three Poems*, 70
Assemblage (of desire), 80
Autobiographical element in poetry, 15, 16, 18–20

Baudrillard, Jean: *In the Shadow of the Silent Majorities*, 84
Benjamin, Walter, 88, 108
Bishop, Elizabeth: "The Map," 70–71
Bloom, Harold, 28
Bove, Paul A.: *Destructive Poetics*, 51–52, 62
Brecht, Bertolt, 105

Cage, John, 83
Cixous, Helene, 80
Cornell, Joseph, 66

Deleuze, Gilles, 91; *Dialogues*, 80; "Rhizome," 89
Derrida, Jacques: *Of Grammatology*, 77; *Margins of Philosophy*, 52
Dine, Jim, 25, 88, 89
Discontinuity, 13, 23–25, 27, 31, 37–49, 67, 90, 92

Eliot, T. S.: *Four Quartets*, 50; "The Love-Song of J. Alfred Prufrock," 105; *The Waste Land*, 16, 88, 92
Ellman, Mary, 68
Erotic poetry, 18, 23, 31, 34, 68–87, 95–99, 101–2, 110

Foucault, Michel, 52
Freud, Sigmund, 54

Graham, Jorie: "Three Poets Wondering Who They Are," 14
Guattari, Felix, 80, 91; "Rhizome," 89

Hedjuk, John, 33
Heraclitus, 108

Johns, Jasper, 17, 25–26, 48, 52, 56, 70, 71, 83
Johnson, Barbara: *The Critical Difference*, 14
Johnson, Lyndon, 20

Kennedy, John, 106
King, Martin Luther, 106
Koch, Kenneth, 15, 17, 27, 28
Koethe, John: "Freely Espoused," 24–25

Lacan, Jacques, 80
"Language Poets," 50, 113
Lowell, Robert: *Life Studies*, 15
Lyotard, Jean-Francois: *The Postmodern Condition*, 29, 51

McGann, Jerome J.: "The Importance of Being Ordinary," 27
Mallarme, Stephane, 37, 45
Miller, Stephen Paul: "Jasper Johns

and David Shapiro, an Analogy," 15, 18, 23
Mondrian, Piet, 25, 26

"New York School of Poetry," 27
Nixon, Richard, 106–7, 109

O'Hara, Frank, 15, 17, 27, 28; "Personism: a Manifesto," 54
Olson, Charles: *The Maximum Poems*, 50
Ophelia *(Hamlet)*, 96, 102–3, 104–5

Padgett, Ron, and David Shapiro, *An Anthology of New York Poets*, 27
Parnet, Claire: *Dialogues*, 80
Pasternak, Boris, 105
Patriarchal authority, critique of, 63, 73, 74, 75, 78, 85, 86–87
Porter, Fairfield, 17, 108
Postmodernism, 29–30, 51

Rauschenberg, Robert, 48, 83
Reading, problematics of, 14, 40–41, 49, 114
Representation: critique of, 50–67, 111–14; origin, originality, translation of, 56–63; totalization of, 63–67; unmediated perception and mediation of, 52–56, 70–75, 114
Rhizome, 89
Rimbaud, Arthur, 105

Shakespeare, William, 16, 112; *Hamlet*, 96, 103, 104, 105; *Othello*, 98
Shapiro, Daniel (poet's son), 36
Shapiro, David: as art critic, 25–26; beginnings as poet, 16; childhood, 16–17; graduate work and book on Ashbery, 25, 28–30; as parent, 36; relation to architecture, 33; statements on relations of poetry and political commitment, 22–23; as student political protester, 20–22; as violinist, 16, 18–20. Works discussed: "About this Course," 30–31, 91, 97; *After a Lost Original*, 36, 56–63, 82–87; "After a Lost Original," 36, 56–63, 67, 81; "Answers to Odd-Numbered Problems," 35; "The Blank Wall," 35; "A Book of Glass," 35; "Canticle," 18; "The Carburetor at Venice," 28; "Commentary Text Commentary Text Commentary Text," 33, 44–49, 100; "The Counter-Example," 34; "The Cures of Love," 30, 83, 96; "December," 35; "The Devil's Trill Sonata," 31–32, 88–110, 112; "Doubting the Doubts," 13, 14, 45; "An Exercise in Futility," 33, 34, 69, 70–75, 87, 110; "Falling Upwards," 18–20; "A Family Slide," 30; "Father Knows Best," 30; "Fire and Life," 28; "A Fragile Art," 27, 35; "Friday Night Quartet," 34–35, 93; "The Heavenly Humor," 39–41, 49, 92, 110; *House (Blown Apart)*, 13, 14, 35–36, 63–67; "The Human Voice," 23; "In Memory of Your Body," 23; Interview (with author, unpublished), 17, 22–23, 31, 97; *January*, 17–18, 22, 68–69, 101; "January," 68–69, 70; *Jasper Johns Drawings 1954–1984*, 25, 26, 56; *Jim Dine: Painting What One Is*, 25, 88, 89; *John Ashbery: An Introduction to the Poetry*, 15, 28–30, 37–38, 41, 70; *Lateness*, 31–32, 34, 44, 51, 61, 88–110; "Lateness," 32; "Life without Mind," 30; "The Lost Golf Ball," 35, 63–67; "Mallarmé to Zola," 33; *A Man Holding an Acoustic Panel*, 13, 27–28, 30, 44; "A Man Holding an Acoustic Panel," 27–28; "Master Canterel at Locus Solus," 24; "Memory of the Present," 34; "Music Written to Order," 32; "Necessity," 28; "The Night Sky," 30, 83, 96; "Ode to Visibility," 28; "On Becoming a Person," 16; *The Page-Turner*, 16, 30–31, 44; "Poem for John Dean," 36; *Poems from Deal*, 22, 23–25, 39–41, 42–43, 44; "Poems from Deal," 24, 42–43, 92, 110; *Poets and Painters: Lines of Color*, 25, 37; "A Prayer," 35; "R's Dilemma," 30; "The Seasons," 36; "Seraphita," 23; "Snow," 13–14; "A Song," 34, 75–82, 87, 110; "A Spanish Painting," 33; "Star," 13, 28; "Study of Two Late July Fourths," 35–36; "Thin Snow," 33; "To a Muse," 35; *To an Idea*, 13, 14, 18–20, 33–35, 44, 53–56, 57, 70–82, 93, 112; "To an Idea," 33, 53–56, 57, 65, 67; "To a Swan," 36; "To a Young Exile," 27, 33–34; "To the

Earth," 27, 33; "To the Page," 33; "Tracks," 24; "Two-Four Time," 30; "Valediction Capricien," 34; "Work in Sadness," 27, 36; "You Are Tall and Thin," 82–87, 110
Shapiro, Frieda (poet's mother), 16, 93–94
Shapiro, Irving (poet's father), 16
Shapiro, Lindsay Stamm (poet's wife), 25
Shelley, Percy Bysshe: "Ode to Liberty," 100; "Ozymandias," 70; "Prometheus Unbound," 100
Simulation, 84–85

Sledge, Percy, 75–76
Stevens, Wallace, 15, 51, 112; "The Man with the Blue Guitar," 50; "Notes Toward a Supreme Fiction," 50, 52–54, 55, 56, 61–62; "An Ordinary Evening in New Haven," 50; "The Snow Man," 54
Stokowski, Leopold, 16

Value in poetry, 111–14
Vertov, Dziga, 103–4

Williams, William Carlos, 68; *Paterson*, 50